JN315980

一日のすべてを英語で表現してみる

毎日少しずつ聴いて、つぶやいて英語に触れる

曽根田憲三
Kenzo Soneda

ブルース・パーキンス
Bruce Perkins

はじめに

　英語上達の切り札は日常的に英語にふれることです。英語の辞書を片手にお気に入りの小説や新聞、雑誌を多読するのも一つの有効な方法。ただし、これらには言語そのものに備わった最も重要、かつ基本的機能である音声がありません。では、映画のDVDはどうでしょう。私たちの心をときめかす世界の美男美女ばかりか、音声付の多くのしゃれたセリフがあります。画面の中で躍動する彼らのまぶしい姿は私たちの心を奪って離しません。しかも使われているセリフと音声は、その場や状況、役柄に最もふさわしいものになっています。とはいえ、彼らの口をついて出る表現は、あまりにもオーセンティックであるために、省略形は言うに及ばず、スラングやジャーゴンなどに満ち溢れたもの。上級者には最適でも初級者や中級者には、しばしば難解なものと映るでしょう。

　英語を母語とする友人を作るとか、日本人同士で英語を話すという方法もあります。ただし、残念ながら、誰もがこうした機会に恵まれるわけではありません。しかも英語で話し合うという方法は一見、容易に思えますが、実はハードルの高い困難が伴うもの。それを実行するには自分だけでなく、他人にも頼らざるを得ないからです。ネイティブスピーカーの友人や英語を話し合う友人がいなければ、また友人が英語を話すのを止めてしまえば、この学習法は成り立ちません。どんな分野の学習もそうですが、最

終的に頼るべきは他人ではなく、自分自身なのです。

　そこで、自分の一日の行動や出来事、あるいは見たり、感じたりしたことを英語で表現するという方法を提案したいと思います。これなら他人に頼ることなく、自分一人で、また誰でも、いつでも容易に実行できるでしょう。朝、目を覚ましたときから、夜、寝床に就くまでの多種多様な行動、動作、遭遇する出来事や状況、頭の中を駆け巡る思いや考えを、きれい事だけではなく、心の奥底で感じた人前では口にできないことも含めて、英語で表現してみることです。たしかに、それら全てを英語で言い表すことは思ったほど簡単ではないでしょう。「だめじゃないか、そんなことしちゃあ」とか「まいったな、財布にお金が入ってない」といった、日常的に使っている日本語表現を即座に英語で言えるでしょうか。でも、それを可能にしてくれる英語表現集さえあれば、誰にでも簡単にできるはず。しかも、この心と体の日常的体験を英語で表現するというやり方は、いつ使うともわからない会話が収められた会話本と異なり、誰もが毎日、繰り返し体験するものであるだけに、興味や記憶の定着を含めた学習効果の点で最も優れた、超お勧めの方法です。そのことは、私たちが母語である日本語を獲得してきた過程を振り返ってみれば明らかでしょう。

　このような理由から、本書はワンランク、ツーランク・アップを熱望する初級者、中級者向けの英語上達の切り札として、朝の目覚めから深夜の就寝中の夢に至るまで、一日の平均的な体験と、そのときの状況ならびに人知れず心の中で感じている思いに関する様々な表現を「描写表現」「つぶやき表現」「SOS表現」

に分類し、国際化たけなわの時代に夢の実現を目指して生きる英語学習者に供するものです。

　なお本書の執筆に際し、会社内での出来事やOA機器に関する表現をより実際的なものにするために、キヤノン（株）知的財産技術センター光学機器知的財産部部長ならびに映画英語アカデミー学会理事の平 純三氏の協力を得ました。記して感謝の意を表します。

　最後に、本書には学習者の便宜を考慮し、次のような工夫がなされています。

- 日本語表現に対応する英語表現が複数ある場合は　/　で区切って、それらの表現を載せています。
- ほぼ同じ意味、同様の意味合いで使われる単語や語句がある場合は　＝　で示しています。
- 同じ意味ではないが、類似した意味合いで使われるものは　→　で示されています。

曽根田憲三

一日のすべてを英語で表現してみる
CONTENTS

Chapter 1　朝　Morning / a.m.　12

目を覚ます、起きる　12	寝不足　16
目覚まし時計　12	十分な睡眠　16
SOS 表現　14	布団・ベッド　18
起きる時間　14	窓を開ける　18
起きたくない　14	エアコン　20

トイレ　20	目の化粧　32
SOS 表現　22	唇の化粧　32
手を洗う　22	化粧について　34
SOS 表現　22	ツメの手入れ　34
洗面所　22	ツメの状態　34
洗面所で　24	衣服を着る　36
歯磨き　24	朝食事　36
シャワーを浴びる　26	コーヒー　38
うがい　26	トースト　38
洗顔　28	サンドイッチ　40
頭髪　28	卵料理　40
髪のセット　30	食欲について　42
化粧　30	

朝刊を読む　42	天気予報　46
経済　42	温度　48
社会　44	その他の表現　50

　　　One Point Lesson　wake up と get up
　　　One Point Lesson　Give me a break

のんびりする　52	ペットの世話　54
植物の世話　52	

　　　One Point Lesson　しまった
　　　One Point Lesson　熟睡する

外出の準備　56	車の場合　62
外出する　58	運転中　64
横断歩道　60	道路　68
自転車の場合　60	違反行為　68
バスの場合　62	事故　70

6

駐車	70		

駅に到着	72	暑い	78
切符を買う	72	寒い	80
改札口	74	事故	80
プラットフォーム	74	社内広告	80
電車に乗る	74	電車SOS	82
電車の中	76	電車を降りる	82
混んでいる	76	乗り換える	82
空いている	78	電車SOS	84
座る	78	改札口を出る	84

One Point Lesson　run out
One Point Lesson　wrinkle

会社で	86	通達	86
会社到着	86	書類	86
持ち場	86		

One Point Lesson　卵について
One Point Lesson　青信号

学校で	90	授業	90
学校	90	遅刻	92

One Point Lesson　wear はこんな風に使われる
One Point Lesson　お茶をいれる

家事	92	布団	100
掃除	92	その他の表現	102
風呂掃除	94	庭掃除	102
台所掃除	94	ガーデニング	102
雑巾	94	その他の表現	104
ゴミ	96	料金の支払い	104
洗濯	96	銀行	106
その他の表現	98	節約	108
乾燥	100		

健康	110	その他の表現	110
栄養	110		

Chapter 2　昼　Noon　112

昼食	112	予算	114
出前を取る	114	味	116
食欲	114		

7

One Point Lesson	降りる
One Point Lesson	ブレーキを掛ける
One Point Lesson	Go faster, man
One Point Lesson	speed

Chapter 3　午後　Afternoon　120

コンピュータ	120	保存する	122
電源を入れる	120	画像処理	122
検索	120	メール	122
入力	120	メール SOS	124
ソフトを使う	120	アプリケーション	124
作成	120	アイコン	126

One Point Lesson	be supposed to
One Point Lesson	節約する

プリンター	128	コンピュータ SOS	130
その他の表現	128	その他の表現	132
互換性	130	ブログ	132

会社で	134	スマートフォン	140
電話	134	ファックス	142
電話の内容	134	ファックス SOS	144
伝言	136	コピー	144
その他の表現	136	コピーSOS	146
電話 SOS	138	郵送する	146
携帯電話	138	時間指定	148
その他の表現	140		

One Point Lesson	小遣い
One Point Lesson	財布いろいろ

会議について	148	企画	152
その他の表現	150		

部下・同僚について	152	性格〈否定的〉	156
性格〈肯定的〉	152	能力〈否定的〉	156
能力〈肯定的〉	154		

他社と交渉	156	契約	160
紹介	158	報告	160
名刺にてついて	158	クレーム	162
商談	160	約束 SOS	162

勤務	162	楽しくない	164
勤務時間	162	その他の表現	166
勤務成績	164	出張	166
楽しい	164	休憩時間	168

給料	170	ボーナス	174
給料日	172	その他の表現	176
安い	172	昇給	176
高い	174	休暇	178
平均的	174		

One Point Lesson　papers と document
One Point Lesson　給料
One Point Lesson　理由について

学校で	182	ノート	188
授業中	182	授業中のおしゃべり	188
授業終了	184	試験	190
その他の表現	184	その他の表現	192
授業中	186	宿題	192
質問	186	その他の表現	196

One Point Lesson　seat について
One Point Lesson　ゴミ

散歩	198	写真	202
その他の表現	198	デート	204
計画	200	愛の告白	204
デートする	200	その他の表現	206
チケット	202	喧嘩	208

One Point Lesson　食欲について
One Point Lesson　手元に

健康	210	熱	216
病院	210	喉	218
検査	210	咳	218
体調	212	風邪	218
眠り	212	歯	218
気分	214	便秘	220
胃	214	体重	220
腰	214	血圧	220
目	214	その他の表現	220
耳	216	肌	222
頭	216	その他の表現	222

One Point Lesson　歯について
One Point Lesson　「痛み」の種類
One Point Lesson　風邪をひく
One Point Lesson　お金にまつわる諺

Chapter 4　夕方　Evening　226

退社する　226

料理　228
献立　228
料理について　228

料理する　228
夕食　230

下ごしらえの表現　230
洗う　230
むく　230
取り除く　230
切る　232
水を切る　232
その他の表現　232
焼く　234
煮る　236
揚げる　236
炒める　236
SOS表現　238
ゆでる　238
卵料理　238
まぜる　240

味付け　240
味　242
おいしい　242
まずい　242
コク　242
調理失敗　242
調理器具　244
火　244
炊く　246
温める　246
冷やす　246
その他の表現　246
給仕　248
その他の表現　248
冷蔵庫　248

One Point Lesson　「長所」を英語で言うと
One Point Lesson　turn on

虫について　252
クリーニング　252

SOS表現　254

買い物　254
店内　256
古い　258
賞味期限　258
衣料品売り場　260
色　260
デザイン　260
サイズ　262
値段　262

高い　262
安い　264
どこの製品　264
SOS表現　264
プレゼント　264
値切る　266
セール　266
会計　268
支払う　268

10

お釣り	268	詰める	270
クレジットカード	268	その他の表現	270
ビニールバッグ	268	ネット注文	270

休日	272	音楽を聴く	278
TV	272	写真を撮る	278
面白い	274	DVDを観る	280
コマーシャル	276	役者について	280
面白い番組	276	ストーリー	280
面白くない	276	歌について	282
録画	278	読書	282
TVゲーム	278		

    One Point Lesson　「思い切って」の英語表現
    One Point Lesson　pupilとstudent
    One Point Lesson　名刺は英語でbusiness card
    One Point Lesson　すねをかじる

外食	286	その他の表現	292
注文	286	支払	294
飲み物	288	チップ	294
食べる	288	持ち金	296
その他の表現	290	SOS表現	296
レストラン	290	頼んでない	296
サービス	290	食べ物について	298
レストランについて	292	その他の表現	298

    One Point Lesson　in the worldについて
    One Point Lesson　make itについて

Chapter 5　夜　Night　300

帰宅	300

夜食	300	その他の表現	302

化粧落とし	302	布団	306
風呂	302	睡眠	306
シャンプー	304	夢	308
湯に浸かる	304	その他の表現	308
風呂から出る	304		

11

Chapter 1 朝

描写表現 目を覚ます、起きる　　　　　　　　　　CD①② 01

私はいつも早く目が覚める。

私は早起きです。

最近はときどき早く目が覚める。

私は朝6時には目が覚める。

私は毎日7時には起きる。

私は7時に目を覚ますが、また寝てしまう。

私は目覚まし時計で目を覚ます。

私はいつも母に起こしてもらう。

私は妻に起こしてもらわないと目が覚めない。

私は朝早く起きられない。

私は8時頃にベッドから起き上がる。

私は朝寝坊です。

描写表現 目覚まし時計　　　　　　　　　　　　CD①② 02

目覚まし時計が鳴り出す。

目覚まし時計が鳴っている。

目覚まし時計の音がうるさい。

目覚まし時計の音がとまった。

つぶやき表現 目覚まし時計

この音うるさいな。

Morning/a.m.

Descriptive expressions — **Waking up**

I always wake up early.

I wake up early. / I'm an early riser.

I wake up early sometimes recently.

I wake up at six in the morning. ⇨ in the morning=a.m.

I wake up at seven every day.

I wake up at seven, but I go back to sleep.

I wake up to an alarm clock. ⇨ wake up to=wake up with

I always get awakened by my mom. / My mother always wakes me up.

If my wife doesn't wake me up, I don't wake up.

I can't wake up early in the morning.

I get up from bed around eight. ⇨ around=about

I oversleep in the morning. ⇨ in the morning=in the mornings

Descriptive expressions — **Alarm clock**

The alarm goes off. ⇨ alarm=alarm clock ⇨ goes off=rings

The alarm clock is ringing.

The alarm clock's sound is noisy. ⇨ noisy=annoying

The alarm stopped ringing. / The alarm clock's sound stopped.

Mumblings — **Alarm clock**

This sound is noisy. ⇨ noisy=irritating

13

いつまで鳴っているの。

いい加減、止まってくれ。

音を切っちゃえ。

> つぶやき表現　**SOS 表現**

目覚ましの音が鳴らないな。

もう目覚ましの音が鳴ってもいい頃だけど。

目覚まし時計をセットするのを忘れていた。

時間を間違えてセットしているよ。

この時計は止まっているじゃないか。

> つぶやき表現　**起きる時間**　　　　　　　　　CD①② 03

今、何時だ？

もう 7 時か。

まだこんな時間か。

もう起きる時間だな。

よし、起きるぞ。

1、2、3 で起きよう。

10 数えたら起きるぞ。

今すぐ起きないと大変だ。

> つぶやき表現　**起きたくない**

起きたくないな。

もう少し寝ていたいよ。

あと 10 分だけ寝よう。

How long is it gonna ring? ⇨gonna=going to ⇨ring=go off

Give me a break.

I'm gonna cut off the sound. ⇨cut off=turn off

Mumblings　SOS expressions

This alarm clock doesn't go off.

It's about time for the wake-up to go off. / It's almost time for the alarm to ring.

I forgot to set the alarm. ⇨set the alarm=set my alarm

I set the wrong time.

This clock's stopped.

Mumblings　Time to get up

What time is it now? / What time is it?

It's already seven o'clock? / Is it seven o'clock already?

It's still only this hour? ⇨this hour=this time

It's time to get up.

Okay, I'm gonna get up. ⇨gonna=going to

I'm gonna get up on one, two, three.

When I count to ten, I'll get up.

I have to get up right now! ⇨ have to=must
⇨ right now=right away

Mumblings　Don't want to get up

I don't wanna get up. ⇨wanna=want to ⇨get up → wake up

I wanna sleep a little more. ⇨a little more=a bit longer

I'll sleep just ten more minutes. ⇨ ten more minutes=ten minutes more

15

もうそろそろ起きないとマズイな。

もうこんな時間じゃないか。

しまった、寝過ごした。

10分だけ寝るつもりが30分も寝ちゃったよ。

会社遅刻しちゃう。

今日は完全に遅刻だな。

ま、いいか。

何かもっともらしい言い訳を考えとこう。

つぶやき表現　寝不足　CD①04

まだ眠い。

今日は3時間しか寝ていない。

昨夜は全く眠れなかった。

今日は寝不足だ。

最近はよく眠れない。

つぶやき表現　十分な睡眠

昨夜はよく寝た。

十分睡眠をとったので疲れが取れた。

近頃は眠くてしょうがない。

I guess I have to get up soon.

It's already this time! ⇨ this time ⇨ this late

Oh no! I overslept! / Damn! I've overslept.

I had only intended to sleep for ten minutes, but I slept for thirty.

I'll be late for work. / I'm gonna be tardy at the company.

Today, I'm totally late. ⇨ totally= completely ⇨ late=tardy

Oh well, that's OK.

I'll think up a plausible excuse.
⇨ think up a plausible excuse=think of a likely pretext

Mumblings — Lack of sleep / Sleep deprivation

I'm still sleepy.

I've only slept three hours today. / I slept only three hours today.

I couldn't sleep at all last night. ⇨ couldn't → didn't

I'm sleep deprived. / I'm suffering from lack of sleep. ⇨ lack of sleep=sleep deprivation

Recently, I can't sleep well. / I don't sleep well these days.

Mumblings — Sufficient sleep

I slept well last night.

I got enough sleep, so I'm not tired. ⇨ enough=sufficient

Gee, I'm so sleepy these days. ⇨ Gee=Wow

いくら寝ても寝足りないな。

描写表現　布団・ベッド　　　　　　　　　　　　　　CD①② 05

私は布団で寝ている。

私は起きたらすぐに布団をたたむ。

布団をたたんで、押入れに入れる。

私はときどき布団をたたむのをさぼる。

私は万年床です。

私はベッドで寝ている。

ベッドが乱れている。

私は起きたらすぐにベッドを整える。

つぶやき表現　布団・ベッド

このシーツを交換しないといけないな。

枕カバーが汚れている。

今日このシーツを洗濯しよう。

そろそろ布団を干さないとだめだな。

描写表現　窓を開ける　　　　　　　　　　　　　　CD①② 06

部屋の窓を開ける。

カーテンを開ける。

ブラインドを上げる。

窓を開けて、空気を入れ替える。

新鮮な空気を入れるために全ての窓を開ける。

No matter how much I sleep, it's not enough.
⇨ how much=how long

Descriptive expressions — Futon / Bed

I sleep on a futon.

I fold up my futon as soon as I wake up.

I fold the futon and put it in the closet.

Sometimes I don't fold the futon. ⇨ the futon=my futon

I leave my futon on the floor.

I sleep on a bed. ⇨ on a bed=in a bed

My bed's messy. ⇨ messy=a mess

As soon as I get up, I make up my bed.

Mumblings — Futon / Bed

I've got to change these sheets. / I have to change these sheets.

The pillow case is dirty. ⇨ case=cover ⇨ dirty=filthy

I'll wash this sheet today. ⇨ this sheet → these shirts

I guess I'll have to hang out the futon soon. / I'll have to hang out my futon sooner or later.

Descriptive expressions — Opening the window

I open the windows in the room.

I open the curtains.

I raise the blinds.

I open the windows and change the air.
⇨ change the air =change the air out the room

I open all the windows and let in fresh air.

19

雨が降っているので窓を少しだけ開ける。

外から排気ガスが入ってくるので、窓を閉める。

描写表現 **エアコン**

エアコンのスイッチを入れる。

エアコンを冷房にする。

暖房を入れる。

温度を設定する。

温度を25度に設定する。

冷房の温度を26度に設定する。

エアコンを除湿にする。

描写表現 **トイレ**　　　　　　　　　　　CD1 07

トイレへ行く。

私は起きると最初にトイレへ行く。

私はトイレの中で新聞を読む。

トイレはすぐにすませる。

トイレの水を流す。

私はトイレの時間が長い。

私はトイレで物を考えるクセがある。

It's raining, so I open the window just a little.
⇨a little=a bit ; a crack

I close the windows because exhaust fumes get in from outside. ⇨exhaust fumes=exhaust gases; emissions
⇨get in from outside → get in

Descriptive expressions　Air conditioner

I turn on the air conditioner. ⇨air conditioner=AC

I set the air conditioner on cool.

I turn on the heater. ⇨heater=heating

I set the temperature.

I set the temperature to 25 degrees. ⇨to=at

I set the air conditioner to 26 degrees.

I set the air conditioner on dehumidify.

Descriptive expressions　Toilet

I go to the boys' room. ⇨ boys' room=men's room; powder room; ladies' room; restroom; loo; bathroom; toilet; potty

When I get up, the first thing I do is go to the restroom. ⇨When=After

I read the newspaper in the bathroom. ⇨newspaper → newspapers

I don't waste time in the bathroom.

I flush the toilet.

I spend a long time in the bathroom.
⇨a long time=a lot of time

I have a habit of thinking about things in the bathroom. ⇨habit=custom

トイレの中にいると時々良い考えが浮かぶ。

つぶやき表現　**SOS 表現**

トイレの紙がない。

トイレの紙が少なくなってきている。

水が流れない。

水が止まらない。

トイレが詰まった。

困ったな、どうしよう。

描写表現　**手を洗う**　　　　　　　　　　CD① 08

水道の蛇口を開ける。

水で手を洗う。

水道の蛇口を閉める。

タオルで手を拭く。

つぶやき表現　**SOS 表現**

蛇口がうまく閉まらない。

蛇口が壊れちゃった。

水が出ない。

描写表現　**洗面所**　　　　　　　　　　CD① 09

顔を鏡で見る。

鏡に映った顔をじっと見る。

Once in a while, I get a good idea in the bathroom.
⇨ Once in a while=Sometimes   ⇨ a good idea=a great idea

Mumblings SOS expressions

There's no toilet paper.

The toilet paper is running out.

The water doesn't flush.

The water doesn't stop. ⇨ doesn't stop=won't stop

The toilet's clogged up. ⇨ clogged up=stopped up

Oh no, what'll I do? / What can I do?

Descriptive expressions Washing hands

I turn on the faucet. ⇨ turn on=open

I wash my hands with water.

I turn off the water from the spigot.
⇨ turn off=shut off   ⇨ spigot=faucet

I wipe my hands with a towel.

Mumblings SOS expressions

I can't turn off the faucet. / I can't turn off the faucet very well.

The faucet broke. ⇨ broke → is broken

The water's not running. / The water is shut off.

Descriptive expressions Washroom

I see my face in the mirror.

I stare at the face in the mirror for a long time. / I stare at the face reflected in the mirror for a long time.

目の下のくまに気づく。

目の回りの小じわが気になる。

頭髪の白髪が気になる。

頭髪が薄くなったのに気づく。

つぶやき表現　**洗面所で**

ニキビができちゃった。

あれっ、鼻の上にニキビができている。

シワが増えたな。

この顔、少しムクんでる感じがする。

どうしたんだろう、目が腫れぼったいぞ。

こんな所にシミができている。

シミが増えたような気がするな。

これらのシミ、ソバカス、どうにかならないかな。

頭の前の部分の髪が薄くなっている。

いつの間にか白髪になっちゃった。

描写表現　**歯磨き**　　　　　　　　　　CD①② 10

歯を磨く。

I've noticed dark rings under my eyes. ⇨ dark rings=dark circles

I'm concerned about little wrinkles around my eyes.

I'm concerned about grey hair. / I'm worried about my white hair.

I've noticed my hair loss. / I've noticed losing my hair. ⇨ hair loss=losing my hair; going bald

> Mumblings   At washroom

I've got a pimple. ⇨ pimple=zit

Oh, I've got a pimple above my nose.
⇨ Oh=Oh wow   ⇨ above my nose=on my nose

My wrinkles have increased, huh? / I'm getting more wrinkles. ⇨ My wrinkles=The wrinkles ⇨ huh?=haven't they?

This face looks a little swollen. / My face looks a bit bloated.

What happened, my eyes are puffy. ⇨ puffy=swollen

I've got a stain right here. ⇨ stain=blemish
⇨ right here=in this place

I think the stains have increased. / It seems the liver spots have increased.

I hope I can get rid of these stains and freckles.

The hair on the front of my head is getting spare. ⇨ getting spare=is receding

I became grey almost overnight. / I got white haired before I knew it.

> Descriptive expressions   Brushing teeth

I brush my teeth.

25

電動歯ブラシで歯を磨く。

奥歯や歯の裏側まで丁寧に磨く。

歯磨きが終わると口をすすぐ。

描写表現 **シャワーを浴びる**

シャワーを浴びる。

シャワーから出たら、ひげを剃る。

ひげは電気カミソリで剃る。

描写表現 **うがい**

うがいをする。

うがい薬でうがいをする。

塩水で口をゆすぐ。

つぶやき表現 **うがい**

今朝は少し喉が痛い。

なんだか口がネバネバする。

喉風邪を引いたかな。

鈴木君から風邪をもらったようだ。

昨日、しゃべりすぎたのかも知れない。

少し口臭がする。

このうがい薬でうがいしておこう。

I brush my teeth with an electric toothbrush.
⇨ brush=polish

I carefully brush my molars and the back of my teeth.

After I brush my teeth, I rinse.
⇨ I rinse= I rinse out my mouth

> Descriptive expressions **Taking a shower**

I take a shower. ⇨ take a shower=take showers

After I get out of the shower, I shave. ⇨ After=When

I shave with an electric razor.

> Descriptive expressions **Gargling**

I gargle.

I gargle with gargle. ⇨ gargle= mouthwash

I rinse out my mouth with salt water.

> Mumblings **Gargling**

My throat hurts a little this morning. ⇨ a little=a bit

Somehow my mouth feels slimy. ⇨ slimy=sticky

Maybe I've got a cold in my throat.
⇨ a cold in my throat=a sore throat

It seems I've caught a cold from Mr. Suzuki.
⇨ seems=looks like

Yesterday I talked too much, maybe.

I've got a little bad breath. ⇨ bad breath=halitosis

I'll gargle this mouthwash. / I'll gargle some of this gargle. ⇨ mouthwash=gargle

> 描写表現　**洗顔**

顔を洗う。

最初に顔を洗う。

お湯で顔を洗う。

洗顔石鹸で顔を洗う。

洗顔フォームで丁寧に顔を洗う。

顔をふいた後、化粧水をたっぷりぬる。

> 描写表現　**頭髪**　　　　　　　　　　　CD①12

髪が短い。

髪が長い。

髪が伸びている。

髪がカールしている。

髪がボサボサになっている。

髪が乾燥している。

髪が乾燥してぱさぱさになっている。

髪の手入れが悪くて、枝毛になっている。

頭は白髪交じりだ。

髪の毛を洗う。

髪の毛をタオルで拭く。

ドライヤーで髪の毛を乾かす。

ヘアートニックを頭皮にふりかける。

頭皮をマッサージする。

Descriptive expressions Washing the face

I wash my face.

First, I wash my face.

I wash my face with hot water.

I wash my face with face soap.

I wash my face carefully with face foam.

After I wipe my face, I apply lots of lotion.
⇨ wipe =dry ⇨ apply lots of lotion=rub on a lot of lotion

Descriptive expressions Hair on the head

My hair's short. / I've got short hair.

I have long hair. / My hair's long.

My hair's growing. ⇨ growing=getting longer

My hair is curly.

My hair's disheveled. ⇨ disheveled=unkempt

My hair's dry.

My hair's stiff and dry.

I messed up and got split ends.

My hair is streaked with grey.

I wash my hair.

I wipe my hair with a towel. ⇨ wipe=dry

I dry my hair with a hair dryer.

I sprinkle hair tonic on my scalp.

I massage my scalp.

描写表現 **髪のセット**

ドライヤーで髪を乾かす。

ドライヤーを使って髪をセットする。

ブラッシングしながらドライヤーでブローする。

コテを使って髪を巻く。

カーラーで髪を内巻きにする。

髪にウエーブをかける。

ヘアーアイロンで髪をまっすぐにする。

ヘアーワックスを塗る。

ヘアースプレーをかける。

つぶやき表現 **髪のセット**

今日は前髪を前にたらそう。

思い切ってオールバックにしてみようかな。

なかなかうまくセットできないな。

白髪が増えてきてるな。

描写表現 **化粧**　　　　　　　　　　　CD①13

化粧水をつける。

乳液をたっぷりつける。

下地のクリームを顔全体に塗る。

化粧をする。

薄化粧をする。

> Descriptive expressions ## Setting one's hair

I dry my hair with a hairdryer.

I use a hairdryer to set my hair.

I blow with my dryer while brushing. / I blow it with my dryer while I brush.

I use a curling iron to curl my hair.

I curl my hair inside with a curler.

I wave my hair. / I make my hair wavy.

I straighten my hair with a hair iron.

I use hair wax. ⇨ hair wax=pomade

I spray on my hair. / I use hairspray.

> Mumblings ## Setting one's hair

I'm gonna wear my hair in bangs today. / I'm going to hang down in front bangs today.
⇨ wear my hair= wear my forelocks

I think I'll wear my hair straight back.

I can't set it very well.

My hair is graying. / My hair is turning grey.

> Descriptive expressions ## Make-up / Cosmetics

I put on lotion. ⇨ put on=apply

I put on a rich milky lotion. / I apply lots of milky lotion on my face.

I apply a base cream all over my face.

I wear makeup.

I wear light makeup.

厚化粧をする。

ファンデーションを塗る。

ニキビを隠すためにコンシーラーを塗る。

頬にチークを塗る。

香水を付ける。

紫外線対策として日焼け止めクリームを塗る。

描写表現 **目の化粧**

アイシャドーを塗る。

黒のアイラインを描く。

目をパッチリ見せるために黒のアイラインを入れる。

まつ毛にマスカラを塗る。

付けまつげをする。

ビューラーでまつ毛を上向きにカーブさせる。

眉毛を描く。

眉毛を整える。

描写表現 **唇の化粧**

リップクリームを塗る。

口紅を塗る。

薄いピンクの口紅をぬる。

唇をセクシーに見せるためにグロスを塗る。

I wear heavy makeup.

I apply foundation.

I apply concealer to hide pimples. ⇨pimples=zits

I wear rouge. / I apply rouge.

I wear perfume.

I apply sunscreen to protect against UV waves.
⇨UV waves=ultraviolent radiation

Descriptive expressions Eye make-up

I apply eye shadow.

I draw on black eyeliner.

I put on black eyeliner to make my eyes look big.
⇨look big=look bigger

I apply mascara to my eyelashes.

I use false eyelashes. ⇨use=wear

I curl up my eyelashes with an eyelash curler.

I draw my eyebrows.

I prepare my eyebrows. ⇨prepare=make up

Descriptive expressions Lip make-up

I use lip cream. ⇨use=wear

I wear lipstick. / I use lipstick.

I apply light pink lipstick.

To make my lips look sexy, I wear lip gloss.

つぶやき表現　化粧について

今日は薄化粧にしよう。

気分転換に厚化粧にしてみようかな。

今日はスッピンでいいや。

今日はしっかりメイクをしよう。

今日は遠出をしないから、薄化粧でいいや。

今日は化粧ののりが悪い。

描写表現　ツメの手入れ　CD❶ 14

ツメの手入れをする。

ツメを切る。

ツメを磨く。

ヤスリでツメを磨く。

ツメの形を整える。

赤のマニキュアを塗る。

気分に合わせてマニキュアの色を変える。

描写表現　ツメの状態

ツメが伸びている。

ツメが欠けている。

ツメの色が悪い。

マニキュアがはげかけている。

Mumblings About make-up

I'll wear light make-up today. / I'll make up lightly today.

I'll wear heavy make-up to change my mood.

I'll go bare faced today. / I'll go without make-up today.

I'm gonna wear proper makeup today. / I'm gonna make up well today.

I'm not going far today, so I'll wear light makeup.

Makeup is not going well on my face today.

Descriptive expressions Nail care

I do my nails.

I trim my nails.

I polish my nails.

I polish my nails with a nail file.

I shape my nails. / I arrange the shape of my nails.

I wear red fingernail polish. ⇨fingernail polish=nail polish

I change the color of my nails to suit my mood.
⇨to suit= to match

Descriptive expressions The condition of fingernails

My nails are long. / My nails have grown long.

My nails are split.

My nail color is bad. ⇨bad=no good

My nail polish is wearing off. ⇨wearing off=chipping off

35

マニキュアが少しはげている。

描写表現　衣服を着る　　　　　　　　　　　CD①② 15

服を選ぶ。

服を着る。

背広を着る。

シャツを着る。

シャツのボタンをはめる。

ズボンをはく。

ジッパーを上げる。

ベルトをしめる。

ネクタイをしめる。

ジャケットを着る。

つぶやき表現　衣服を着る

どの服にしようかな？

今日は少しおしゃれをしよう。

よし、今日はこのドレスに決めた。

このジャケットには何色のネクタイが似合うかな？

今日はノーネクタイにしよう。

描写表現　朝食時　　　　　　　　　　　CD①② 16

朝食の準備をする。

やかんに水を入れる。

湯を沸かす。

My nail polish is a little worn. ⇨ worn=thin

Descriptive expressions — Wearing clothes

I select my clothes. ⇨ select=choose

I wear clothes. ⇨ wear=put on

I wear a suit.

I put on a shirt.

I button my shirt. ⇨ button=button up

I put on pants. ⇨ pants=trousers; slacks

I zip my zipper. / I zip up.

I put on a belt.

I put on a tie. ⇨ tie=necktie

I wear a jacket.

Mumblings — Wearing clothes

What shall I wear?

I'll dress up a little today.

I've decided on this dress today. / I've decided to go with this dress today.

I wonder what color tie will go with this jacket.

I'll go with no tie today. / I won't wear a necktie today.

Descriptive expressions — Breakfast time

I prepare for breakfast.

I put water in the kettle.

I boil water.

描写表現　コーヒー

コーヒーを入れる。

コーヒーにミルクと砂糖を入れる。

スプーンでよくかき混ぜる。

コーヒーをブラックで飲む。

アイスコーヒーを作る。

コーヒーをコップにそそぐ。

コーヒーを飲む。

つぶやき表現　コーヒー

コーヒーを飲みたい気分だ。

今日はブルーマウンテンを飲もう。

時間がないからインスタントコーヒーにしよう。

コーヒーにしようかな、それとも紅茶がいいかな。

このコーヒーはおいしいな。

このコーヒーは超まずいな。

このコーヒーは濃すぎる。

もう少し薄いコーヒーがいいな。

このコーヒー、熱い。

このコーヒー、生温い。

このコーヒー、冷めちゃってるよ。

描写表現　トースト　　　　　　　　　　　CD①② 17

トーストを作る。

Descriptive expressions Coffee

I make coffee.

I put milk and sugar in my coffee. ⇨ put=take

I stir it well with a spoon.

I drink my coffee black. / I don't put anything in my coffee. ⇨ put=take

I make iced coffee.

I pour coffee into the cup.

I drink coffee.

Mumblings Coffee

I feel like drinking coffee.

Today, I'll drink Blue Mountain.

I don't have time so I'll drink instant coffee.
⇨ drink instant coffee=do instant coffee

Should I have coffee, or maybe go with tea?

This coffee's delicious.

This coffee's terrible. ⇨ terrible=horrible

This coffee's too strong.

I think a little thinner coffee would be better.

This coffee's hot.

This coffee's lukewarm. ⇨ lukewarm=tepid

This coffee's cold.

Descriptive expressions Toast

I make toast. ⇨ make=fix

トースターでパンを焼く。

パンが焼けたかどうかチェックする。

トースターからパンを取り出す。

冷蔵庫からバターとジャムを取り出す。

パンにバターを塗る。

パンにイチジクジャムを塗る。

> つぶやき表現　**トースト**

もう少し焼いた方がいいかな。

トーストをこがしちゃった。

パンにはイチジクジャムが一番だ。

> つぶやき表現　**サンドイッチ**

サンドイッチを作ろう。

最近は野菜不足だ。

レタスとトマトをたっぷり挟もう。

> 描写表現　**卵料理**　　　　　　　　　　　CD❶❷ 18

ゆで卵を作る。

目玉焼きを作る。

スクランブルエッグを作る。

> つぶやき表現　**卵料理**

ゆで具合は半熟がいいな。

ゆで卵は硬めにしよう。

I toast bread in a toaster.

I check to see if the bread's toasted or not.
⇨see if=see whether

I take the toast out of the toaster.

I take out some butter and jam from the fridge.
⇨fridge=refrigerator

I spread butter on my bread.

I spread fig jam on my bread.

> Mumblings　Toast

Maybe it needs to be toasted a bit more.

I burned the toast. ⇨burned=burnt

Fig jam is best on bread.

> Mumblings　Sandwiches

I'll make sandwiches. ⇨make=fix

I'm not getting enough vegetables recently.
⇨getting=eating　⇨recently=these days

I'll put in lots of lettuce and tomatoes. ⇨put in=put on

> Descriptive expressions　Egg dishes

I make boiled eggs.

I make eggs sunny-side-up.

I make scrambled eggs.

> Mumblings　Egg dishes

I like them soft boiled.

I'll make hard-boiled eggs.

41

卵はなんといっても両面焼きだよ。

つぶやき表現　食欲について　　　　　　　　　　　CD①19

今朝は食欲がない。

今朝はなにも食べたくない。

朝食はスキップだ。

ああ、腹減った。

朝からモリモリ食べるぞ。

最近は食欲が出てきた。

季節のせいかな。

いつもは、朝食は食べないが、今日は食べよう。

描写表現　朝刊を読む　　　　　　　　　　　CD①20

新聞を郵便受けへ取りに行く。

新聞を広げる。

最初に新聞の第一面を見る。

新聞の見出しに目を通す。

次に新聞の経済面を開く。

円の為替レートをチェックする。

スポーツ面を開いて昨日の野球の試合の結果を見る。

つぶやき表現　経済

ヨーロッパの経済は大変だな。

It's fried eggs overeasy for me.

Mumblings About appetite

I don't have any appetite this morning. / I'm not hungry this morning.

I don't want to eat anything this morning.

I'll skip breakfast.

Ah, I'm hungry.

I'm gonna eat like a horse from the morning.
⇨ eat like a horse=eat heartily; have a good appetite

I've gotten a good appetite recently. ⇨ good appetite= big appetite

Maybe it's because of the season. ⇨ it's because of= it's due to

I usually don't eat breakfast, but today I will.

Descriptive expressions Reading the morning paper

I go and get the morning paper from the mailbox.

I open the paper.

First, I look at the front page.

I scan the headlines. ⇨ scan=look at

Next, I open to the financial page.

I check the yen exchange rate. ⇨ exchange rate= exchange rates

I open the sports page and look at last night's baseball results. ⇨ open=turn to

Mumblings Economy/Economics

European economies are in trouble. ⇨ are in trouble=are having a hard time

日本の経済は上向きだ。

いつまで円高が続くんだろう。

もう少し円安になってほしいよ。

今日も１ドル７０円だ。

この調子だと１ドル６０円になるんじゃないか心配だ。

せめて１ドル１００円になってほしいね。

つぶやき表現　　**社会**

日本の社会もぶっそうになってきたな。

最近は暗い事件ばかりだ。

また殺人事件だ。

最近はストーカー殺人事件が多いな。

警察の不祥事が増えているな。

学校でのいじめが一向に減らないね。

交通事故による死者が多い。

実に怖い世の中になったものだ。

世の中、一体どうなっているんだ。

The Japanese economy is picking up. ⇨ picking up= turning up

I wonder how long the strong yen will continue.
⇨ continue=last

I'd like to see a little weaker yen. / I'd like the yen to be a little bit weaker.

Today one dollar is already 70 yen.

At this rate, I'm worried it will go to 60 yen to a dollar. / I'm concerned it will become one dollar for 60 yen. ⇨ I'm worried =I'm concerned

I'd like to see it go to 100 yen to the dollar.

Mumblings Society

Japanese society has become dangerous.

Recently, there have been only dark incidents.
⇨ dark=dismal

There's been another homicide. ⇨ homicide=murder

There have been many stalking murders recently.

Police scandals are increasing. / Disgraceful police incidents are increasing.

Bullying at schools hasn't gone down at all.
⇨ hasn't gone down=hasn't decreased

There are a lot of traffic fatalities in traffic accidents. ⇨ traffic fatalities=traffic deaths

We're living in a really scary world. / The world has become really frightening. ⇨ frightening=scary

What's the world coming to? / What's happening to the world?

夜、独りでは歩けないね。

もっと楽しいニュースはないのかな。

明るい社会になってほしいものだ。

描写表現 **天気予報**　　　　　　　　　　　　CD①②21

天気予報を見る。

天気予報で日本各地の天気をチェックする。

天気予報で地球の温暖化を知る。

つぶやき表現 **天気予報**

明日も雨か。

今日は午後から雨の予報だ。

明日の予報は曇り後雨だ。

2日連続で雨だ。

最近は曇りの日が多いな。

晴れて欲しいね。

今日も熱帯夜だよ。

暑くて夜、眠れない。

予報によると、明日の午後は35度を超えるってさ。

At night, you can't walk by yourself. / You can't walk alone at night.

Why can't the news be more enjoyable? ⇨ enjoyable= fun

I hope society becomes brighter.

> Descriptive expressions   Weather forecast / Weather report

I watch the weather report.

I check the weather forecasts all over Japan.
⇨ all over Japan=throughout Japan

I learn about global warming on the weather report.

> Mumblings   Weather forecast / Weather repor

Rain again tomorrow, huh?

Rain is forecast for this afternoon. / It's gonna rain this afternoon.

Tomorrow's forecast is cloudy followed by rain.

It's rained for two days. / It's been raining for two days in a row.

There have been a lot of cloudy days lately. / It's been cloudy a lot recently.

I hope it clears up. ⇨ clears up=gets fine

It's gonna be a tropical night today, too.

It's hot and I can't sleep at night. / It's so hot so I can't get to sleep at night.

According to the report, it will be over 35 degrees tomorrow afternoon.

熱射病にかからないように水分の補給が必要だな。

最近、天気予報はずっと外れているからな。

今日の予報は当たるかな。

描写表現　温度　　　　　　　　　　CD❶22

温度計で部屋の温度をチェックする。

今、部屋の温度は30度だ。

温度計は32度を示している。

この部屋の温度は5度しかない。

湿度計を見る。

湿度は70%。

つぶやき表現　温度

暑いな。

蒸し暑い。

少し動くだけで汗が出る。

湿度が高すぎて気持ちが悪い。

ああ、寒い。

凍えそうだ。

今がちょうどいい温度だな。

You need to rehydrate to avoid heat exhaustion.
⇨ rehydrate=replenish your water ⇨ avoid =prevent
⇨ heat exhaustion=heatstroke

The weather forecasts have been wrong a lot lately.

I wonder if today's forecast will be right.
⇨ will be right= will happen

> Descriptive expressions   Temperature

I check the room temperature with a thermometer.

Now, the room temperature is 30 degrees.

The thermometer says 32 degrees. ⇨ says=shows

The temperature in this room is only 5 degrees.
⇨ in=of ⇨ only=just

I look at the hydrometer.

The humidity is 70 percent.

> Mumblings   Temperature

It's hot.

It's muggy.

If I move around even a little, I sweat.

The humidity is too high, so I don't feel good.

Ah, it's cold.

I'm gonna freeze. ⇨ freeze=get a chill

Now is the perfect temperature. / The temperature is just right.

部屋の温度は22度、申し分ないね。

快適な温度だ。

描写表現 その他の表現　　　CD①② 23

新聞のチラシをチェックする。

スーパーのチラシを見る。

チラシで野菜の値段を調べる。

肉の値段が一番安い店を探す。

バーゲンセールをチェックする。

つぶやき表現 その他の表現

ここのスーパーは安いな。

A店とB店ではどっちが安いかな。

どこかバーゲンセールをしている店はないかな。

牛肉はこのスーパーが安い。

このスーパーの日用品はどこよりも安い。

今日はこの店へ行ってみることにしよう。

One Point Lesson wake up と get up

　　wake の基本的な意味は to stop sleeping、言い換えれば to become awake です。すなわち、眠りや夢などから「覚める、目を覚ます」ということ。一方、get up は「起き上がる」の意。そのため I get up at 6 o'clock. とすると「私は6時に起床します」、つまり目を覚まし、「寝床から出る」ということを表します。

50

The room temperature is 22 degrees. Perfect. / The room temperature is 22 degrees; it's just right.

It's a comfortable temperature.

_{Descriptive expressions} **Other expressions**

I check newspaper leaflets. ⇨leaflets=inserts

I look at the supermarket leaflets.

I look up vegetable prices in the leaflets.
⇨look up=search for

I look for the shop with the cheapest meat prices.
⇨shop=store

I check for bargain sales.

_{Mumblings} **Other expressions**

This supermarket is cheap. ⇨cheap=cheaper

I wonder which is cheaper, A store or B store.

Maybe some store is having a bargain sale.

This store's beef is cheap.

This supermarket's daily necessities are cheaper than anywhere else. ⇨daily necessities=daily necessaries; daily commodities

I think I'll go to this store today. ⇨go to=check out

One Point Lesson _{Give me a break}

この表現は Please give me a chance、Please give me another chance、I have had enough、Drop this matter、Stop bothering me. などの意を表すイディオム。つまり、嘆願したり、困惑したり、いらだったときなどに「頼むよ、もう一度チャンスをくれ、いい加減にしろ、よせよ」といった意味合いで使われる便利な表現です。

描写表現 **のんびりする**

何もしないでのんびり過ごす。

一日中家でゴロゴロする

昼まで寝ている。

描写表現 **植物の世話**　　　　　　　　　　CD①24

テラスの花に水をやる。

ポットの花に朝と夕方、水をやる。

鉢植えの花に肥料をやる。

花に防虫スプレーをかける。

花柄(かへい)をつむ

庭の花をつむ。

花を花瓶に活ける。

椿を剪定(せんてい)する。

つぶやき表現 **植物の世話**

この花、元気がないな。

昨日は元気だったのに、今日はしおれている。

今日は綺麗に咲いている。

このバラ、明日は咲きそうだ。

新芽が出ている。

アブラムシが付いている。

この毛虫を退治しないとだめだ。

花が台無しになったのは、この虫が原因だな。

Descriptive expressions Taking it easy

I spend time just doing nothing.

I lie around all day at home. / I idle away time at home all day.

I sleep till noon.

Descriptive expressions Plant care

I water the plants on the terrace. ⇨ terrace=veranda

I water the potted flowers in the mornings and evenings. ⇨ potted flowers=flower pots

I fertilize the potted flowers.

I spray the flowers with bug spray. ⇨ bug spray=insecticide

I pick peduncles.

I pick flowers in the garden. ⇨ in the garden=from the yard

I arrange flowers in a vase. ⇨ vase=flower pot

I trim the camellias.

Mumblings Plant care

This flower's not healthy. ⇨ not healthy=not looking good

Yesterday it was fine and today it's withered. ⇨ withered=wilted

Today it's in magnificent bloom. ⇨ in magnificent bloom=blooming beautifully

This rose looks like it'll bloom tomorrow. ⇨ bloom=blossom

New buds are growing out. ⇨ buds=sprouts

It has aphids. /There are aphids on it.

I have to get rid of these caterpillars. ⇨ get rid of=exterminate

What ruined these flowers are these bugs.
⇨ ruined=spoiled ⇨ bugs=insects

この枝を切り取ろう。

昨日、水をやったから今日はいいか。

描写表現　ペットの世話

ペットに餌をやる。

ポチを抱く。

犬の頭をなでる。

犬を散歩につれて行く。

いつものルートを散歩する。

犬の糞を始末する。

描写表現　ペットの世話

ポチが餌を欲しがる。

ポチが鳴く。

ポチが言うことをきかない。

ポチが私の命令を無視する。

ポチが散歩に行きたがる。

ポチがボール遊びをしている。

One Point Lesson　しまった

　私たちは物事をし損なったり、うっかりして忘れたりした際の当惑や嫌悪、あるいは苛立ちなどを表す時に「しまった」「まいったな」などといった言葉をしばしば口にしますが、それらに対応する英語はたくさんあります。
　「おやおや、なんだって」といった驚きを表す Goodness, Goodness gracious、驚き、軽いののしり、不審などを表す Gosh, By gosh、当惑、嫌悪、怒りなどを表す Damn, Damn it, Dash it, Hang it, Hang it all。damn ほど下品ではない Confound it などがよく使われます。

I'll cut off this branch. ⇨ cut off=trim

I watered it yesterday, so it's OK today.
⇨ it's OK today=I don't have to today

Descriptive expressions — Pet care

I feed my pet.

I hold my Pochi. ⇨ hold=cuddle

I pet the dog's head.

I walk my dog. / I take my dog for a walk.

We walk the same route.

I clean up the dog's poop. / I clean up after the dog. ⇨ clean up=dispose

Descriptive expressions — Pet care

Pochi wants food. / Pochi's hungry.

Pochi barks.

Pochi doesn't listen to me. ⇨ listen to me=obey me

Pochi ignores my commands.

Pochi wants to go for a walk.

Pochi is playing with a ball.

One Point Lesson 　熟睡する

　この意を表す一般的な表現は sleep well です。しかし、sleep soundly、sleep heavily、またイディオムを使って I slept like a log. (熟睡したよ) といった具合に sleep like a log、sleep like a top などともします。また I fell into a deep sleep. のように fall into a deep sleep、fall into a profound sleep とすることも可能です。なお、「熟睡している」のように状態を表す場合は He is fast asleep. といった具合に be fast asleep とします。なお fast に代わって sound、dead も OK。

描写表現　外出の準備

窓を閉める。

窓に鍵をかける。

カーテンを閉める。

ブラインドを下ろす。

部屋の電気を消す。

ガスの元栓を閉める。

テレビを切る。

テレビの電源コードを抜く。

鞄の中身をチェックする。

必要な書類が入っているかどうか確認する。

ズボンと上着のポケットを調べる。

財布の中身を確認する。

車のカギを探す。

花粉症対策としてマスクをする。

靴を磨く。

折り畳みの傘を鞄に入れる。

傘を持って玄関を出る。

玄関のドアのカギをかける。

つぶやき表現　外出の準備

戸締りは大丈夫かな？

Descriptive expressions ## Prepare for going out

I close the windows.

I lock the windows.

I close the curtains. ⇨curtains=drapes

I lower the blinds.

I turn off the lights in the room.

I turn off the gas. / I turn off the gas at the main cock.

I turn off the TV.

I pull the plug on the TV. / I pull the TV plug.

I check inside my bag.

I make sure whether I put in my necessary papers.
⇨make sure=confirm ⇨whether=if ⇨papers=documents

I check my trouser and jacket pockets.

I confirm the contents of my wallet. / I make sure what's in my purse. ⇨wallet=billfold

I look for my car keys.

I wear a mask to protect from pollinosis. / I wear a mask to counter hay fever. ⇨hay fever=pollen allergy

I polish my shoes.

I put my folding umbrella in my bag.

I take an umbrella and go out the front door.

I lock the front door.

Mumblings ## Prepare for going out

I wonder if I locked the door.

忘れ物はないかな？

ポケットに財布は入っているかな？

1万円で足りるかな？

財布は空っぽじゃないか？

今日は傘を持って行ったほうがよさそうだな。

今日は傘はいらないだろう。

描写表現 **外出する**　　　　　　　　　　CD①27

家を出る。

学校へ行く。

仕事に行く。

勤務先へ行く。

隣の人に挨拶をする。

途中で近所の人から声をかけられる。

駅に向かう。

小走りで駅に向かう。

最寄りのバス停まで歩く。

つぶやき表現

急がないと遅刻だ。

もう少し早足で歩こう。

走らないと遅れる。

Did I forget anything? / Have I forgotten something?

Is my wallet in my pocket? / Did I put my wallet in my pocket?

Is 10,000 yen enough? / Will ten thousand yen be enough?

My wallet isn't empty, is it?

It looks like I should take an umbrella today.

I probably won't need an umbrella today.

> Descriptive expressions **Going out**

I go out.

I go to school.

I go to work.

I go to my workplace.

I greet my neighbors.

On my way, I am greeted by a neighbor. ⇨ am greeted= am spoken to

I head for the train station.

I scurry for the station. / I trot off heading for the station.

I walk to the closest bus stop.

> Mumblings

If I don't hurry, I'll be late.

I'll walk a little faster.

If I don't run, I'll be late.

描写表現 **横断歩道**　　　　　　　　　　　　CD①28

横断歩道で信号待ちをする。

信号が青に変わるのを待つ。

イライラする。

信号が青になったので、横断歩道を急いで渡る。

信号無視して渡る。

つぶやき表現 **横断歩道**

赤信号かよ。

今日はついてないな。

早く青に変わってくれよ。

信号が変わるのが遅いんだよ。

電車に遅れちゃうじゃないか。

今は黄信号だ。

よし、渡っちゃえ。

描写表現 **自転車の場合**　　　　　　　　　CD①29

自転車に乗る。

自転車で駅まで行く。

自転車のペダルをこぐ。

自転車のブレーキをかける。

自転車をとめる。

自転車を下りる。

自転車を自転車置き場に置く。

Descriptive expressions Crosswalks

I wait for the light to change at crosswalks.

I wait for the signal to turn green.

I get irritated. ⇨ irritated=upset

I hurry across the crosswalk because the light turned green.

I walk against the light. / I ignore the light and cross.

Mumblings Crosswalks

It's a red light?

I'm having a bad day. / It's a bad hair day.

Come on, turn green already.

This light takes a long time to change.

I'm going to be late for the train.

The signal's yellow now.

OK, let's cross. ⇨ cross=go across

Descriptive expressions By bicycle

I ride a bike. ⇨ bike=bicycle

I take a bike to the station. ⇨ station=train station

I pedal the bicycle.

I brake the bike.

I stop the bike.

I get off the bike.

I park the bike in the bicycle parking lot.
⇨ park=put ⇨ parking lot=parking area

描写表現　バスの場合　　　CD①30

バスを待つ。

バスに乗る。

バスの座席に座る。

バスの中で立つ。

バスが揺れるので、吊革につかまる。

つぶやき表現　バスの場合

バスが来ないな。

このバスは遅いな。

もう5分遅れているじゃないか。

いったい、いつになったらバスは来るんだ。

このバスは7時10分にくるはずなんだけど。

まいったな。

描写表現　車の場合　　　CD①31

駐車場に行く。

車のドアを開ける。

タイヤを調べる。

車に乗り込む。

車のドアを閉める。

エンジンをかける。

車の窓を開ける。

Descriptive expressions **By bus**

I wait for the bus.

I get on the bus.

I sit down on the bus. ⇨the bus=the bus seat

I stand in the bus.

The bus sways, so I hold onto a strap.
⇨sways=rocks ⇨hold onto=get

Mumblings **By bus**

The bus is taking a long time. / The bus is taking a long time to get here.

This bus is late.

It's already 5 minutes late, isn't it?

When in the world will the bus get here?
⇨get=come; arrive

Isn't this bus supposed to be here at seven ten?
⇨to be here=to get here

Damn! ⇨Damn=Crap ; Shoot

Descriptive expressions **By car/ By automobile**

I go to the parking lot.

I open the car door.

I check the tires.

I get in the car.

I shut the door. ⇨shut=close

I start the engine.

I open the car windows.

車の中の空気を入れ替える。

車の窓を閉める。

座席を調整する。

シートベルトを締める。

冷房を入れる。

暖房を入れて、26度に設定する。

バックミラーを覗く。

車の左右を確認する。

車を出発させる。

つぶやき表現　車の場合

タイヤが少しぺしゃんこになっているな。

空気圧が低いな。

タイヤがすり減っている。

エンジンの調子が悪いな。

エンジンがかからない。

バッテリーがあがったみたいだ。

1か月もこの車、使っていなかったからなあ。

描写表現　運転中　　　　　　　　　　CD① 32

車を運転する。

大通りを直進する。

法定スピードで運転する。

I change the air in the car.

I close the windows.

I adjust my seat.

I fasten my seatbelt.

I turn on the air conditioner.

I turn on the air conditioner and set it to 26 degrees. ⇨set it to=set it for

I glance at the rearview mirror. ⇨glance at=take a peek at

I check to the left and right of the car.

I start off. / I take off.

Mumblings — By car/ By automobile

The tire's a little low, isn't it? ⇨low=flat

The air pressure is low, isn't it?

The tire's worn. ⇨worn=worn down

The engine's in bad condition. / Something's wrong with the engine. ⇨in bad condition=in poor condition

The engine won't start. ⇨start=turn over

The battery seems to be dead. / The battery seems to have died.

I didn't use this car in a month, did I? ⇨didn't use=haven't driven

Descriptive expressions — While driving

I drive a car.

I proceed on highways. ⇨proceed=go through
⇨highways=boulevards; main streets

I follow the speed limit. / I drive at the posted speed.

細い通りを時速４０キロ以下で走る。

スピードを落とす。

安全運転する。

徐行運転する。

第２車線を走る。

スピードを上げる。

高速道路をスピードを出して走る。

急カーブを曲がる。

カーブで徐行運転する。

右折するためにウインカーを出す。

ウインカーを出して、左に曲がる。

ブレーキをかける。

前の車が突然停車したので、急ブレーキをかける。

クラクションを鳴らす。

のろのろ運転の車を追い越す。

ライトをつける。

> つぶやき表現　**運転中**

渋滞が始まったぞ。

ここは渋滞が激しいな。

この場所はいつも渋滞している。

不思議にも、今日は交通量が少ないな。

I drive under 40 kilometers per hour on narrow streets. ⇨drive under=drive below ⇨streets=roads

I slow down. / I decelerate.

I drive safely. / I'm a safe driver.

I drive slowly. ⇨drive slowly=slow down

I drive in the second lane.

I speed up. / I accelerate.

I drive fast on the freeway.

I go around big curves. ⇨go around=turn around

I drive slowly in curves. / I slowdown in curves.
⇨in curves=for curves

I signal to turn right. / I turn on the right signal.

I turn on the signal and turn left.

I brake. / I step on the brake.

The car in front of me braked suddenly, so I used the parking brake. ⇨used the parking brake=hit the emergency brake

I sound the horn. / I beep the horn.

I overtake a slow moving car.

I turn on the lights. ⇨turn on=put on

Mumblings While driving

The traffic jam has started. ⇨started=begun

This is a bad traffic jam. ⇨bad=gridlocked

This place is always a traffic jam.

Strangely, there's little traffic today.
⇨Strangely=Mysteriously; Unusually

あれっ、意外と空いているじゃない。

前の車、のろのろ運転しているな。

もっと早く走ってよ。

ウインカーも出さないで、車線変更するなって。

危ない、急ブレーキをかけるのはやめてくれ。

描写表現　道路

国道を走る。

途中で高速道路に入る。

料金所でお金を払う。

ETCで料金を払う。

描写表現　違反行為

CD①②33

違法運転をする。

猛スピードで運転する。

スピード違反をする。

30キロオーバーのスピード違反をする。

飲酒運転をする。

駐車違反をする。

信号無視をする。

ウインカーを出さないで右折する。

一方通行を逆走する。

一時停止の交通標識を無視する。

Hey! It's unexpectedly traffic free. ⇨traffic free=open

The car in front is going really slow, isn't it?
⇨going=being driven

Go faster, man.

Don't change lanes without signaling. ⇨change=turn

Watch out! Don't jam on the brakes.

Descriptive expressions ▸ Route

I take the national highway. ⇨take=drive ⇨highway=route

I get on the freeway along the way.

I pay the toll at the tollgate.

I pay by ETC. ⇨ETC=Electric Toll Collection System

Descriptive expressions ▸ Traffic violations

I drive illegally. / I don't follow traffic rules.
⇨traffic rules=traffic laws

I drive really fast. / I drive at high speed.

I drive over the speed limit. / I speed.

I drive 30 kilometers an hour over the limit.
⇨over the limit=over the speed limit

I drive drunk. / I drive under the influence of alcohol.

I commit parking violations.

I run red lights. / I ignore the red light.

I turn right without signaling.

I drive the wrong way on one-way streets. ⇨drive=go

I ignore stop signs.

路肩を走る。

警官につかまる。

警官にチケットを切られる。

描写表現　事故

交通事故を起こす。

前の車に追突する。

後続車に追突される。

自転車と接触事故を起こす。

警察に電話で連絡する。

描写表現　駐車　CD①②34

職場に到着する。

駐車場に着く。

駐車場所を探す。

指定の駐車スペースに車を止める。

駐車スペースがない。

駐車する場所がない。

つぶやき表現

どこへ停めたらいいのかな？

駐車場所がないじゃないか。

駐車場はないのかな？

少しの時間だから、ここ停めちゃえ。

I drive on the shoulder. / I drive on the shoulder of the road.

I get caught by the police.

I get tickets from the police.

Descriptive expressions **Accidents**

I have traffic accidents. ⇨have=cause

I hit the car in front. ⇨in front=ahead of me

I get hit from behind.

I have accidents contacting bicycles. ⇨contacting=hitting

I call the police. ⇨call=phone

Descriptive expressions **Parking**

I get to work. / I arrive at work.

I get to the parking lot. ⇨parking lot=car park

I look for a parking space. / I look for a place to park. ⇨parking space=parking spot

I park in a reserved parking space. ⇨reserved=designated

There's no parking space.

There's nowhere to park.

Mumblings

Where should I park?

There's no place to park, is there?

I wonder if there's a parking space.
⇨if=whether ⇨parking space=parking lot

It's just a short time, so I'll stop here.
⇨It's just a short time=It'll only be a little while

71

道路際に車を停めよう。

警察は来ないだろう。

描写表現　駅に到着　　　CD①② 35

駅に着く。

駅の階段を上る。

エスカレータに乗る。

エレベータで上がる。

改札口へ向かう。

描写表現　切符を買う

チケット売り場へ行く。

自動販売機でチケットを1枚買う。

チケットを買うために列に並ぶ。

間違ったチケットを買う。

定期券が切れている。

乗車カードをチャージする。

つぶやき表現　切符を買う

乗車券が高いな。

東西駅まで800円だって？

この路線の乗車券は他に比べて高い。

乗車券を間違って買っちゃった。

I'll park at the side of the road. ⇨park at=park by
⇨road=street

Maybe a police officer won't come. ⇨police officer=cop

> Descriptive expressions Getting to the station

I get to the station.

I go up the station steps.

I get on the escalator. ⇨get on=take

I take the elevator up.

I head for the ticket wicket. ⇨ticket wicket=ticket gate

> Descriptive expressions Buying a ticket

I go to the ticket sales counter. ⇨ticket sales counter → ticket sales machine

I buy a ticket at the vending machine.

I stand in line to buy a ticket. / I queue up to buy a ticket.

I buy the wrong ticket.

My train pass has expired. ⇨expired=run out

I recharge my train pass.

> Mumblings Buying a ticket

Tickets are expensive, aren't they? / The price of tickets is high, huh?

It's 800 yen for Tozai Station?

Tickets on this line are expensive compared to other lines. ⇨on this line=for this line
⇨compared to=compared with

I bought the wrong ticket by mistake.

２０円高い乗車券を買っちゃったよ。

払い戻してもらわないと。

今日で定期券が切れる。

帰りに新しい定期券を買うことにしよう。

描写表現　改札口　CD①36

改札口でチケットを機械に入れる。

改札口で定期券をタッチする。

改札口を通過する。

描写表現　プラットホーム

上り線のプラットホームに向かう。

階段を下りて目的地へ向かう電車のホームに向かう。

プラットホームで電車が来るのを待つ。

女性専用車両が停止する位置へ歩いて行く。

描写表現　電車に乗る

電車に乗り込むために２列に並ぶ。

時間ぴったり。

電車に乗り込む。

各駅の電車に乗り込む。

急行電車に乗る。

I bought a ticket for 20 yen too much. / I paid 20 yen too much for the ticket.

I'll have to get a refund.

My train pass expires today.

I'll buy a new train pass when I go home.
⇨ go home=go on my way home

Descriptive expressions Ticket wicket / Ticket gate

I put the ticket in the ticket wicket machine.

I touch the ticket gate with my train pass.

I go through the ticket wicket.

Descriptive expressions Platform

I head for the platform for up trains. ⇨ head for=go to
⇨ up trains=trains going toward Tokyo

I go down the steps and head for the platform for my destination. ⇨ steps=stairs

I wait on the platform for my train to come.

I walk to the Ladies Only stop position. / I walk to the Women Only stop area.

Descriptive expressions Getting on the train

We line up in two rows to get on the train. / We stand in two lines to get on the train.

It's just on time. / It's right on time.

I get on the train.

I get on a local train.

I take an express train.

描写表現　電車の中

席を探す。

空いた席を見つける。

席に座る。

すぐ降りそうな人の前に立つ。

シルバーシートを探す。

シルバーシートに座る。

年配の人が乗ってきたので席を立つ。

年配の人に席を譲る。

網棚に鞄を載せる。

吊革につかまる。

ドアに寄り掛かる。

つぶやき表現　混んでいる

混んでいるな。

超満員じゃないか。

混んでいて息苦しいよ。

この線はいつも混んでいる。

人が多すぎるんだよ。

押すなよ。

寄り掛かるなよ。

よし、こいつに寄り掛かってやろう。

あっ、こいつ、足を踏んだな。

これだからラッシュアワーの電車は嫌いなんだ。

Descriptive expressions **On the train / In the train**

I look for a seat.

I find an empty seat.

I sit on a seat.

I stand in front of someone who looks like he's going to get off soon. ⇨ he's → she's

I look for a priority seat.

I sit on the priority seat.

I stand up when an elderly person gets on.

I give my seat to elderly people. ⇨ give=give up

I put my bag on the luggage rack. ⇨ luggage rack= luggage shelf

I hold onto a strap. ⇨ hold onto=grab

I lean against the door.

Mumblings **Crowded**

It's crowded, isn't it?

It's packed, isn't it? ⇨ packed=overcrowded

It's crowded and hard to breathe.

This line is always crowded.

There are too many people.

Don't push. ⇨ push=shove

Don't lean on me.

Well, I'm gonna lean on him.

Hey, that guy stepped on my toes. ⇨ guy=person

I hate rush hour because it's like this.

> つぶやき表現　**空いている**

今日はめずらしく空いている。

この電車はガラガラだな。

空いた席はないかな。

あっ、あそこが空いている。

他の人に座られちゃった。

> つぶやき表現　**座る**

この目の前の人、早く降りてくれないかな。

この人、新聞を閉じたぞ。

どうやら次の駅で降りそうだな。

よし、あの人の前に立とう。

やっと座れる。

今日は運がいい。

座席が狭いな。

この人、もう少し詰めてくれないかな。

この人、2人分の座席を取っているじゃないか。

座席に荷物は置くなって。

自分の膝の上に置いてほしいよ。

> つぶやき表現　**暑い**　　　　　　　　　　　CD①②38

蒸し暑いな。

冷房が全然きいてない。

これじゃあ車内より外のほうが涼しいよ。

Mumblings **Empty**

Today, it's empty for a change.

This train is empty.

I wonder if there are any empty seats.

Oh, there's an empty seat over there.

Somebody else sat down. ⇨Somebody else=Someone else

Mumblings **Sit on a seat**

I hope the person in front of me gets off soon.

This person folded up his newspaper. / This person closed the newspaper.

It looks like he's going to get off at the next stop.
⇨he's → she's ⇨stop=station

Well, I'll stand in front of that person.

Finally, I can sit down.

I'm lucky today.

The seat's narrow, isn't it?

Won't this person scoot over a bit more? ⇨scoot over =pack in

Isn't this person taking up two seats? ⇨taking up= occupying

Don't put packages on the seat. ⇨packages =bags

I want people to put them on their laps.

Mumblings **Hot**

It's muggy, isn't it?

The air conditioner isn't working at all.

It's cooler outside the train than inside.

79

> つぶやき表現　　**寒い**

少し寒い。

冷房が効きすぎだ。

> つぶやき表現　　**事故**

少し遅れている。

人身事故があったって言っている。

事故のせいで電車が大幅に遅れているってさ。

車両事故のために運転を停止しているだって。

電車の運転を見合わせるだって？

早く運転を再開してくれよ。

もう１時間も待ってるんだ。

運転再開の見込みはないだって？

どうやって家に帰ったらいいんだ？

今日は台風のせいで電車は不通だ。

> つぶやき表現　　**車内広告**　　　　　　　CD①② 39

何か面白い広告はないかな。

いろんな広告があるな。

Mumblings Cold

It's a little cold.

The air conditioning is too cold.

Mumblings Accident

It's a little bit late.

They say someone jumped in front of the train. / They say there was a traffic accident resulting in personal injury. ⇨ the train → a train

The trains are widely late due to an accident. / Trains are late all over because of an accident.

They say the trains are stopped due to a traffic accident. ⇨ traffic accident：車両を含めた幅広い交通事故。車両のみの事故は railroad accident

Are they postponing the trains? ⇨ postponing=delaying

Come on, get the train going again. ⇨ going=running

I've already been waiting an hour. ⇨ an hour=one hour

They don't know when the train will start running again?

How should I go home? / What's the best way to get home?

The trains aren't running today due to a typhoon.

Mumblings Advertising in the train car

I wonder if there are some interesting advertisements. / Aren't there any interesting ads?

There are a lot of advertisements.

週刊誌の広告は刺激的だな。

あれっ、あれはわが社の広告だ。

わが社の飲料水の広告が壁に貼ってある。

描写表現　電車SOS

電車が揺れる。

電車が揺れて、人に押される。

電車が急ブレーキをかける。

人に足を踏まれる。

偶然、人の足を踏む。

その人ににらまれる。

その人に謝る。

描写表現　電車を降りる

CD①②40

網棚から鞄を下ろす。

電車を降りる。

いつもの駅で降りる。

次の駅で降りる。

急いで電車から降りる。

下りるときに後ろから押される。

描写表現　乗り換える

階段を上る。

電車を乗り換える。

隣のプラットホームへ移動する。

The weekly magazine ads are stimulating.

Oh, there's our company's advertisement.

Our company's drinking water ad is on the wall.
⇨ is on the wall=is posted on the wall

Descriptive expressions Train SOS

The train rocks. / The train sways.

The train rocks and I get pushed.

The train brakes suddenly.

My feet get stepped on.

I step on a person's feet accidentally. ⇨ feet → foot

The person stares at me.

I apologize to the person.

Descriptive expressions Getting off the train

I take down my bag from the luggage rack.
⇨ luggage rack=luggage shelf

I get off the train.

I get off at the usual station. ⇨ the → my
⇨ usual=regular

I get off at the next stop. ⇨ stop=station

I hurry and get off the train.

I get pushed as I get off the train. ⇨ as=when

Descriptive expressions Transferring

I go up the stairs. ⇨ stairs=stairway; steps

I change trains. / I transfer trains.

I move to the next platform.

反対側のプラットホームへ行く。

別の電車に乗る。

東京行きの電車に乗る。

東京行きの電車に乗り換える。

各駅列車に乗り換える。

描写表現　**電車ＳＯＳ**

電車に乗り遅れる。

いつもの電車に乗り損ねる。

電車の中で居眠りをする。

居眠りしていて、降りる駅を乗り過ごす。

急いで目的の駅へ引き返す。

描写表現　**改札口を出る**

改札口を出る。

Ａ４出口へ向かう。

One Point Lesson　run out

　この表現の基本的意味は He ran out of the room.（彼は部屋から走り出た）のように「走って出る、飛び出す」です。Time ran out before I could answer the question.（私がその質問に答える前に時間切れになった）、My money ran out.（お金が底をついた）のように、時間、金、物資、忍耐などについては「無くなる、尽きる」を意味します。

I go to the opposite side platform. / I go to the other side of the platform.

I get on another train. / I take another train.

I get on a train for Tokyo. / I take an up train.
⇨ an up train（上り列車）→ a down train（下り列車）

I transfer for a train for Tokyo. ⇨ for Tokyo=to Tokyo

I change to a local train.

Descriptive expressions Train SOS

I miss the train.

I miss my usual train. ⇨ my → the

I fall asleep on the train. ⇨ on the train=in the train

I fall asleep and go past my station. ⇨ go past=ride past

I hurry up and catch a train back to the station.

Descriptive expressions Going out the ticket wicket

I go out the ticket wicket. ⇨ ticket wicket=ticket gate

I head for exit A4.

One Point Lesson wrinkle

　この語は本来なめらかな面であるべきところにできた「しわ」、人間に使われると皮膚、特に顔の「しわ」を意味します。This shirt is full of wrinkles.（このシャツはしわだらけだ）のように、布や紙などの「しわ」にも頻繁に使われます。なお、Don't wrinkle your skirt.（あなたのスカートにしわをつけないように）と、動詞として用いても結構です。

会社で

描写表現 **会社到着**　　　　　　　　　　　　CD❶②41

オフィスビルに到着する。

エントランスカードを使ってゲートを入る。

会社に到着する。

守衛に挨拶する。

エレベータに乗る。

エレベータで5階に行く。

タイムカードをタイムレコーダに通す。

描写表現 **持ち場**

同僚に挨拶をする。

笑顔で同僚の挨拶を返す。

自分の職場に到着する。

自分の席に着く。

描写表現 **通達**

朝礼をする。

部下に関連事項を伝える。

部下に指示を出す。

部下から報告を受ける。

描写表現 **書類**　　　　　　　　　　　　CD❶②42

机の上の書類に目を通す。

At office

Descriptive expressions — Getting to work

I get to the office building. ⇨ the office building= my office building

I use my entrance card and go in the gate.

I get to work. / I get to my office. / I get to the company.

I greet the guard. ⇨ guard → guards

I take the elevator. / I get in the elevator. ⇨ get in= get on

I take the elevator to the 5th floor.

I punch my time card.

Descriptive expressions — Workplace / Work station

I greet my colleagues. ⇨ colleagues=co-workers

I smile and return my colleagues greetings.

I get to my workplace.

I get to my desk.

Descriptive expressions — Notices

I have a morning assembly. ⇨ assembly=meeting

I tell my subordinates related things. ⇨ things=details
⇨ related things → informative things ; messages

I give notices to my subordinates. ⇨ subordinates= underlings

I get reports from my subordinates. ⇨ get=receive

Descriptive expressions — Documents

I glance at documents on my desk. / I look at papers on my desk. ⇨ glance at=look at

机の引き出しを開ける。

引き出しから書類と筆記用具を取り出す。

今日のスケジュールをチェックする。

会議のための書類を作成する。

書類に必要事項を書き込む。

書き込んだ内容を確認する。

誤字や脱字をチェックする。

書類に印鑑を押す。

書類を上司に提出する。

書類に上司の印鑑をもらう。

契約書にサインする。

One Point Lesson　卵について

　1個の卵は an egg、「生卵」は a raw egg、an uncooked egg です。「新鮮な卵」は a fresh egg、「生みたての卵」は a newly-laid egg、「卵の殻」は an eggshell、「卵の白身」は the white of an egg、「卵の黄身」は the yellow of an egg、the yolk of an egg といいます。調理した卵「ゆで卵」は a boiled egg、「落とし卵」a poached egg、「半熟卵」a soft-boiled egg、「固ゆで卵」a hard-boiled egg、「いり卵」scrambled eggs、「目玉焼き」sunny side up です。

I open my desk drawer.

I take out documents and writing implements from my drawer.

I check today's schedule.

I make documents for meetings.

I write down necessary items on the documents.

I confirm what I've written. / I check the contents of what I wrote.

I check for misspellings and omissions.

I put my personal seal on the documents.
⇨ documents=paper

I give the documents to my superior. ⇨ superior= senior; boss

I get my boss's seal on the documents. / I have my senior put his seal on the documents.
⇨ his seal → her seal

I sign contracts.

朝・午前

昼

午後

夕方

夜

One Point Lesson　青信号

　Wait until the light turns green.（信号が青になるまで待ちなさい）のように、信号機の「青」は blue ではなく green。それもそのはず、私たちが「青」で表現している信号の色は「緑」だからです。つまり、英語の場合は信号の色に忠実というわけですね。では、なぜ日本では「緑」と言わないで「青」というのでしょうか。それは、日本人は古来より野山の緑色の葉を「青葉」というように、「緑」を「青」と表現してきたからです。ちなみに辞書で「青」を調べると「緑」という意味が含まれています。

89

学校で

描写表現　学校　　　　　　　　　　　　　　　CD①43

学校に到着する。

教室に入る。

教室を間違える。

教室を探す。

描写表現　授業

1時限目の授業に間に合う。

1時限目の授業にどうにか間に合う。

授業に遅刻する。

授業に5分ほど遅刻する。

授業に遅刻して教師にしかられる。

つぶやき表現　授業

どうにか間に合った。

もう少しで遅刻するとこだったよ。

まずい、遅刻だ。

この先生、いつも時間通りに授業を始めるんだ。

まだ先生、出席を取っていないだろうな。

この授業の先生は出席を取らないから大丈夫だ。

At school

Descriptive expressions — School

I arrive at school. / I get to school.

I go into the classroom.

I mistake the classroom. / I go to the wrong classroom.

I look for the classroom.

Descriptive expressions — Class

I get to first period class on time.

I manage to get to first period class on time.

I'm late for class. / I'm tardy for class.

I'm five minutes late for class.

I am scolded by the teacher for being late for class. ⇨ I am scolded → I was scolded ⇨ for class=for the class

Mumblings — Class

Somehow I made it. / Somehow I got here on time. ⇨ I made it=I got here on time.

I was almost late. / I almost didn't make it on time.

Damn, I'm late! ⇨ Damn=Shoot ; Oh no
⇨ I'm late → I'm gonna be late

This teacher always begins his class on time.

Maybe this teacher hasn't finished calling the roll. ⇨ calling the roll=taking attendance

This class's teacher doesn't take attendance, so, I'm good. ⇨ take attendance=call the roll
⇨ I'm good=it's cool

91

描写表現 遅刻　　　　　　　　　　CD❶44

遅刻の理由を聞かれる。

遅刻の理由を述べる。

遅刻の理由をでっちあげる。

遅刻をバスのせいにする。

つぶやき表現 遅刻

なんて言おうかな。

適当な理由を言っちゃおう。

もっともらしい遅刻の理由が思い浮かばないよ。

電車が遅れたことにしよう。

One Point Lesson　wear はこんな風に使われる

　この語の基本的な意味は「身に着けている」。そのため、He wears a coat.（彼は上着を着ている）のように、衣類についてはもちろんのこと、He wears glasses.（彼は眼鏡をかけている）、She wears high heels.（彼女はハイヒールをはいている）、She wears a jewel.（彼女は宝石を付けている）、She wears a perfume.（彼女は香水を付けている）、She wears lipstick.（彼女は口紅を付けている）といった具合に、肌に付ける装身具や化粧品などについても使われます。また顔の表情、様子、態度なども私たちの体に密着していることから、She wears a smile.（彼女は笑みを浮かべている）、He wears an air of triumph.（彼は勝ち誇った態度をしている）のようにも使われています。

家事

描写表現 掃除　　　　　　　　　　CD❶45

部屋を片付ける。

部屋の掃除をする。

Descriptive expressions — Being late

The teacher asks the reason for being late.

I tell why I'm late. / I tell the reason for being tardy.

I make up reasons for being tardy. ⇨ make up=fabricate

I lay the blame on the bus for being late.

Mumblings — Being late

What shall I say?

Maybe I'll say a vague excuse.

I can't think of a plausible reason for being late.
⇨ think of=think up

I'll say the train was late.

One Point Lesson　お茶をいれる

　お茶やコーヒーなどを「入れる」という場合は、文字通りの表現 put in ではなく、make です。そのため、「お茶を入れてくれますか」は Will you make tea for me? とします。なお、make に代わって brew もしばしば使われますので頭に入れておいてください。

　「お茶を注ぐ」は She poured out tea for me.（彼女は私にお茶を注いでくれた）のように pour out、「お茶を出す」は She served me tea.（彼女は私にお茶を出してくれた）のように serve とします。また、「お茶はどう？」と相手の意向を尋ねるときは How about tea?、「お茶を一杯どうですか」は Won't you have a cup of tea?、「お茶にしよう」は Let's have a tea break。ちなみに tea というと black tea（紅茶）を意味しますので、「緑茶」は green tea としてください。

Housework

Descriptive expressions — Cleaning

I tidy up the room. ⇨ tidy up=clean up

I clean the room.

93

テーブルを雑巾でふく。

タンスのほこりを払う。

コンピュータのスクリーンをふく。

コンピュータのキーボードにはたきをかける。

床をモップでふく。

床をワックスでみがく。

ワックスがけした床を、乾いた後、雑巾で軽くふく。

畳に掃除機をかける。

窓ガラスをふく。

描写表現 **風呂掃除**

風呂おけを洗う。

風呂おけにカビ取りスプレーをかけてスポンジでこする。

風呂おけを磨く。

鏡についた水アカをこすって落とす。

描写表現 **台所掃除**

食器を洗う。

洗剤で食器を洗う。

自動食器洗い機で食器を洗う。

描写表現 **雑巾**　　　　　　　　　　　　　CD①② 46

掃除をする際に雑巾を使う。

I wipe the table with a cloth. ⇨cloth=rag

I dust the chest of drawers. ⇨chest of drawers=wardrobe

I wipe the computer screen.

I use a duster on the keyboard. / I dust the keyboard with a duster.

I mop the floor.

I wax the floor. / I wax and polish the floor.

I wipe the waxed floor with a cloth lightly after it's dry.

I vacuum the tatami mats.

I clean the windows. / I wipe the windows.

Descriptive expressions ▶ Cleaning the bath

I wash the bathtub.

I apply mold killer on the bathtub and sponge it.
⇨mold killer=mold spray

I rub the bathtub. ⇨rub=polish

I remove the water scum on the mirror.
⇨water scum=incrustation

Descriptive expressions ▶ Cleaning the kitchen

I wash the dishes. ⇨the dishes → dishes

I wash dishes with dish soap.

I wash the dishes in a dishwasher.

Descriptive expressions ▶ Cloth

I use a cloth when I clean.
⇨cloth=rag   ⇨clean → clean the house

雑巾をバケツの水にひたす。

濡れた雑巾を絞る。

使い終わった雑巾を洗って乾かす。

描写表現　**ゴミ**

ゴミを掃いて集める。

ゴミをゴミ袋に入れる。

ゴミを分別する。

燃やせるゴミと燃やせないゴミを分ける。

ゴミ収集日を確認する。

ゴミを出す。

ゴミを指定の場所へ持っていく。

新聞と雑誌は他のゴミと区別する。

使わなくなったコンピュータをリサイクルに出す。

描写表現　**洗濯**　　　　　　　　　　　　　　　　CD①②47

洗濯する。

洗濯ものを仕分ける。

色のついたものと白の衣服を分ける。

洗濯ものを洗濯機に入れる。

洗濯機のスイッチを入れる。

I soak the rag in a bucket of water.

I squeeze the wet cloth.

I wash and dry the rags I've used.

> Descriptive expressions **Trash / Garbage / Rubbish**

I sweep up the trash.

I put the trash in a trash bag.
⇨ trash bag; garbage bag; bag

I separate the trash. ⇨ the trash → my trash

I separate the trash into nonflammable and flammable trash. ⇨ flammable trash=burnable trash

I confirm trash pick-up days.
⇨ pick-up days=collection days

I take out garbage. ⇨ take out garbage → put out the trash

I go and put the rubbish in the designated spot.
⇨ spot=place

I put newspapers and magazines into different trash.

I recycle computers I don't use anymore.

> Descriptive expressions **Laundry / Washing**

I do laundry. / I wash clothes.

I sort the laundry.

I separate clothes into colors and whites.

I put the laundry into the washer.
⇨ washer=washing machine

I push the washing machine switch. ⇨ push=press

洗濯機に液体洗剤を入れる。

柔軟剤を入れる。

洗濯機の「洗濯」と「乾燥」のボタンを押す。

洗濯ものを乾燥機で乾かす。

洗濯ものをテラスで干す。

つぶやき表現　　洗濯

洗濯ものがずいぶんたまったな。

今日は洗濯しよう。

今日は洗濯日和だ。

このシャツにシミがついている。

このシミ、目立つな。

この靴下に穴があいている。

こんなところが破れているぞ。

赤いシャツと一緒に洗ったから、これ、少し赤くなった。

この服、少し色が落ちたみたいだ。

描写表現　　その他の表現　　CD①② 48

お気に入りのコートにカビが生えている。

湿気で衣服がカビだらけになっている。

ドレスが虫に食われている。

I pour liquid soap into the washer.
⇨ liquid soap=detergent

I add fabric softener. ⇨ add=put in

I press the "Wash" and "Dry" buttons on the washing machine.

I dry the clothes in a dryer.

I dry clothes on the veranda. ⇨ veranda=terrace

(Mumblings) Laundry / Washing

The laundry's really piled up.

I'll wash clothes today. / I'm gonna do the laundry today.

Today is the perfect day for washing clothes.

This shirt's stained. / This shirt has a stain.

This stain is noticeable.

This sock has a hole in it. / These socks have holes.

This part's ripped. ⇨ ripped=torn

I washed this with a red shirt, so it turned a little red.

It looks like the color of this clothing has faded.

(Descriptive expressions) Other expressions

My favorite coat is moldy.

In the moist air, these clothes have become covered with mold. ⇨ moist air=dampness

The dress has been eaten by insects. / This dress is moth-eaten.

99

ズボンが虫に食われて、あちこちに穴が開いている。

つぶやき表現　その他の表現

これじゃあ、もう着られないよ。

防虫剤が無くなっていたんだ。

防虫剤を入れておけばよかった。

さっそく防虫剤を買いに行かないとだめだな。

これらの洋服を虫干ししよう。

描写表現　乾燥

洗濯ものを干す。

洗濯ものが乾いたので、取り入れる。

洗濯ものをたたむ。

シャツにアイロンをかける。

アイロンをかけてズボンのしわを伸ばす。

描写表現　布団　　　　　　　　　　　　CD12 49

布団を干す。

シーツを取り替える。

布団カバーをつける。

毛布をクリーニングに出す。

These trousers have been eaten by insects and have holes all over. ⇨ trousers=pants ⇨ all over=here and there

Mumblings / Other expressions

I can't wear this anymore.

I'm out of insect repellent. / The mothballs have run out.

I should've added insect repellent.
⇨ insect repellent=mothballs

I'll have to go out and buy insect repellent.
⇨ buy insect repellent=buy some insect repellent

I'll air out these clothes.

Descriptive expressions / Dry

I dry clothes. / I'll dry the laundry.

The laundry's dry, so I'll bring it in.

I fold the clothes. ⇨ clothes=laundry

I iron the shirt.

I iron out the wrinkles in these trousers.
⇨ trousers=pants; slacks

Descriptive expressions / Futon

I air out the futon.

I change sheets.

I put on the futon cover.

I have the blanket cleaned. / I send the blanket to the cleaner's.

描写表現　その他の表現

畳を日干しする。

障子を張り替える。

蛍光灯を入れ替える。

電球が切れたので、新しいものと交換する。

描写表現　庭掃除　　　　　　　　　　　　CD① 50

庭を掃除する。

庭をほうきで掃く。

庭の落ち葉を拾い集める。

芝生を刈る。

草取りをする。

芝生の雑草を抜く。

雑草に除草剤をまく。

つぶやき表現　庭掃除

雑草がたくさん生えているな。

雑草が多すぎて取りきれない。

春はすぐいろんな雑草が生えてくる。

描写表現　ガーデニング　　　　　　　　　CD① 51

花を植える。

チューリップの球根を植える。

庭の中央にモミジの木を植える。

Descriptive expressions Other expressions

I sun-dry the tatami mats.

I change the paper on the sliding doors.

I change the fluorescent lights.

The light-bulb's burnt out, so I change the bulbs.
⇨ change the bulbs=put in new bulbs

Descriptive expressions Cleaning the yard

I clean the yard. / I clean the garden.

I sweep the yard.

I collect the fallen leaves in the garden.
⇨ collect=gather ; rake up

I mow the lawn. / I cut the grass.

I weed the garden.

I pull the weeds in the yard.

I sprinkle weed killer. ⇨ sprinkle=spread

Mumblings Cleaning the yard

Lots of weeds have grown. / A lot of weeds are growing.

There are too many weeds to pull out.

In spring, a lot of weeds grow quickly.

Descriptive expressions Gardening

I plant flowers.

I plant tulip bulbs.

I plant a maple tree in the middle of the yard.
⇨ in the middle of=in the center of   ⇨ yard=garden

庭で季節の花を育てる。

植物に肥料をやる。

花に防虫スプレーをかける。

バラのつぼみについたアブラムシを駆除する。

庭の松の木を剪定する。

庭の片隅に植えている玉ネギを収穫する。

ブルーベリーの実を収穫する。

描写表現　その他の表現

ポットの花に水をやる。

花を生けるために、ユリの花を3本切る。

桜の木を植えるために、スコップで庭に穴を掘る。

穴に堆肥を入れる。

描写表現　料金の支払い　　CD①52

新聞代を集金員に払う。

送られてきた請求書に目を通す。

ガス代を払うために銀行へ行く。

通販で買った商品の代金を支払うためにコンビニへ行く。

自動引き落としで水道代を払う。

ATMで家賃を払う。

I grow seasonal flowers in the yard.

I fertilize the plants.

I spray insecticide on the flowers. ⇨ insecticide= insect repellent

I get rid of the aphids on the rose buds.

I trim the pine tree in the yard.

I dig up the onions planted in the corner of the garden. ⇨ dig up=harvest ⇨ corner=nook

I harvest some blueberries. ⇨ some blueberries → the blueberries

Descriptive expressions Other expressions

I water the potted flowers.

To arrange some flowers, I cut off three lilies.

I dig a hole in the ground with a scoop to plant a cherry tree. ⇨ scoop=spade

I put compost in the hole.

Descriptive expressions Pay a fee / Pay charge

I pay the paper deliverer. ⇨ paper deliverer=paperboy

I glance at my bills. / I go over the bills I got sent.

I go to the bank to pay the gas bill.
⇨ the gas bill → my gas bill

I go to the convenience store to pay for some stuff I bought through mail order. ⇨ stuff=goods

I pay my water bill by automatic payment.

I pay my rent at an ATM.

つぶやき表現 料金の支払い

今月の電気代は高いな。

やれやれ、9月から電気代が上がるのか。

来月は水道代を節約しないといけないな。

来月から新聞の購読はやめよう。

ニュースはインターネットで見ればいい。

描写表現 銀行　　　　　　　　　　　　　CD① 53

銀行へお金を下ろしに行く。
口座からお金を下ろす。

自動支払機から1万円を引き出す。

銀行へ預金する。
自動支払機で3万円預金する。
口座の残高をチェックする。

口座には10万円しか残ってないので、ショックを受ける。

つぶやき表現 銀行

手元に2,000円しかない。

毎日、お金が出ていく。

Mumblings Pay a fee / Pay charge

The electric bill is high this month. / This month's electric bill is high.

Boy, the electric bill is going up from September.
⇨ Boy=Wow

I'll have to conserve water for next month's water bill.

I won't subscribe to a newspaper from next month.

I'll read the news on the Internet. ⇨ read the news= check out the news

Descriptive expressions Banks

I go to the bank and withdraw some money.

I take money out of my account.

I take out ten thousand yen from an automatic payment machine. ⇨ an automatic payment machine=an ATM

I save money at the bank.

I save thirty thousand yen at an ATM.

I check my account balance.

I was shocked that there's only a hundred thousand yen left. ⇨ a hundred thousand yen =one hundred thousand

Mumblings Banks

I've got only 2,000 yen with me. / I've only got 2,000 yen on me.

Money goes out every day.

107

今月はあと5,000円で生活しなきゃいけないんだ。

宝くじでも買うとするか。

1等が当たれば1億円だ。

1億円の宝くじが当たらないかな。

描写表現　**節約**　　　　　　　　　　　　　CD❶ 54

家計簿をつける。

出費を抑える。

節約する。

今すぐ必要でないものは極力、買わないようにする。

節電、節水に努める。

エアコンに代わって扇風機を使う。

テレビは1日3時間に制限する。

1か月のこづかいを減らす。

こづかいを5万円から3万円に減額する。

つぶやき表現　**節約**

家中をオール電化にして失敗した。

太陽電池装置をつけようかな。

今月は冠婚葬祭が続いたので、かなり出費した。

給料が少ないので、毎日のやりくりが大変だ。

I have to live on 5,000 yen the rest of the month. ⇨the month=this month

Maybe I'll buy a lottery ticket.

If I hit the first prize, it's one hundred million yen.

I wish I could hit the 100 million yen jackpot.
⇨jackpot=prize

Descriptive expressions   Saving

I keep a household account book. ⇨keep= make

I control what I spend. / I hold down my spending.

I conserve. / I become thrifty.

I try with all my might not to buy things I don't need right away.

I try to conserve electricity and water.

I use a fan instead of air conditioning.

I limit watching TV to three hours a day.

I cut my monthly spending money. ⇨spending money=pocket money

I cut my pocket money from 50,000 yen a month to 30,000 yen.

Mumblings   Saving

It was a mistake to have an all-electric home.
⇨home=house

Maybe I'll put on solar panels. ⇨solar panels=photovoltaic cells

This month I had weddings and funerals, so I spent a lot of money. ⇨spent a lot of money=I had a lot of expenditures

My pay is low, so it's tough to manage with the limited budget every day.

健康

描写表現　栄養

健康には気を付けている。

毎日の食事には十分気を付けている。

バランスの取れた食事を心がけている。

野菜と肉類のバランスに気を配っている。

最近は野菜中心の食事にしている。

野菜をたっぷり取るよう気をつけている。

描写表現　その他の表現

規則正しい生活を心がけている。

睡眠を十分に取るよう心掛けている。

どんなに忙しくても5時間の睡眠は確保している。

夜8時以降の食事は取らないようにしている。

脂っこいものは避けるようにしている。

どんなにおいしくても満腹になるまでは食べないようにしている。

腹八分の食事を心がけている。

Health

Descriptive expressions ### Nutrition

I'm careful about my health.
⇨ about my health=about health

I'm very careful about my food every day.

I take care about getting a balanced diet.
⇨ getting=eating

I'm careful about the balance of vegetables and meat. ⇨ vegetable=veggie; vegie; veggy

Recently, I mainly eat veggies. / I eat mostly vegetables these days.

I'm careful to get plenty of vegetables.

Descriptive expressions ### Other expressions

I'm careful about living a regular life.

I'm careful to get enough sleep.

No matter how busy I am, I always get five hours' sleep.

I try not to eat after eight in the evening.
⇨ eight in the evening=8 p.m.

I try to avoid oily food. ⇨ oily food=fatty food ; greasy food

No matter how delicious it is, I try not to get full. ⇨ get full=get a full stomach

I'm careful to get 80% full. / I try to be moderate in eating. / I never stuff myself.

Chapter 2 昼

描写表現　昼食

昼食を作る。

昼食をとる。

12時30分に昼食をとる。

自分の弁当を食べる。

昼休みに、持参した愛妻弁当を食べる。

12時になると、仕事をやめて社員食堂へ行く。

昼休みに、昼食を食べに外へ出かける。

いつものレストランへ行く。

月曜日は日本食のレストランへ行く。

火曜日にはイタリアンレストランでスパゲティを食べる。

水曜日になると会社近くの中華料理店でラーメン定食を食べる。

今日の昼は野菜中心のAランチにする。

私は早く食べられるのでいつもカレーライスを注文する。

昨日は寿司だったので、今日は焼き肉にする。

Noon

Descriptive expressions — **Lunch**

I make lunch. / I cook lunch. / I prepare dinner.

I eat lunch.

I eat lunch at 12:30.

I eat my lunch.

At lunch break I eat the lunch my dear wife made. ⇨ At=On ⇨ dear=loving

At 12 o'clock, I quit working and go to the cafeteria. ⇨ 12 o'clock=12 noon ⇨ quit working=stop working

At lunch time, I go out for lunch. / During lunch break, I go out to eat lunch.

I go to my usual restaurant. / I go to the regular restaurant.

On Mondays, I go to a Japanese restaurant.

On Tuesdays I go to an Italian restaurant and eat spaghetti.

Thursdays I go to a Chinese restaurant near the company and eat a ramen lunch. ⇨ company=office

Today for lunch I'm going to have the mainly vegetable A lunch. ⇨ mainly=mostly

I always order curry rice because I can eat it fast. ⇨ fast=quickly

Yesterday was sushi, so today I'll have grilled meat. ⇨ have=do ⇨ grilled meat=roast meat ; broiled meat ; Korean barbecue

私はコンビニでおにぎりとお茶を買って食べる。

同僚と近くのコンビニへ弁当を買いに行く。

描写表現　**出前を取る**

昼食を作らないで出前を取る。

電話でピザを注文する。

宅配の寿司を取る。

つぶやき表現　**食欲**　　　　　　　　　　　　　　CD① 57

早いな、もう昼食の時間か。

おなかが空いた。

今日はたくさん食べるぞ。

デラックスランチを2人前だって食べられるぞ。

なんだか全然おなかが空いてないよ。

今日はあまり食べたくないな。

最近は全然、食欲が湧かない。

描写表現　**予算**　　　　　　　　　　　　　　CD① 58

今日は持ち合わせが少ない。

財布には 1,000 円しか入っていない。

昼食には 700 円以上は使えない。

I buy a rice ball and tea at a convenience store and eat that.

I go to a nearby convenience store with a colleague and buy a boxed lunch.
⇨ a colleague → my co-workers

Descriptive expressions Getting a delivery

I don't fix lunch, I get a delivery. ⇨ fix lunch=make lunch

I order a pizza by phone.

I order home delivered sushi. / I order sushi by home-delivery service. ⇨ order=get

Mumblings Appetite

That was fast ; it's already lunchtime. / Time flies. It's lunchtime already.

I'm hungry.

I'm gonna eat a lot today. / I'm gonna pig out today.

I can eat two deluxe lunches.

For some reason, I'm not hungry at all.

I really don't want to eat today.

I don't have much of an appetite these days. / Recently, I don't have an appetite at all.

Descriptive expressions Budget

I don't have much money today.

I've got only 1,000 yen in my wallet. / I've only got a thousand yen in my purse. ⇨ wallet=billfold

I can't spend over 700 yen for lunch. ⇨ over=more than

今日の昼食代は 500 円以下にする。

今日は思い切って 1,500 円のランチにする。

いろんな料理を注文して予算をオーバーする。

つぶやき表現　予算

今日は 600 円前後の昼食にしよう。

本日の予算は 900 円か。

たまには高いものを食べたいな。

1 か月に一度は高級レストランへ行きたいよ。

つぶやき表現　味

B ランチはおいしそうだ。

どの料理もおいしそうだ。

A と B、どっちがおいしいかな？

このインドカレーはとてもおいしい。

この料理の味はまあまあだな。

このミートソースはまずい。

この料理を注文して失敗だった。

Today, I'll spend 500 yen or less for lunch.

Today, I'll be daring and have a 1,500 yen lunch.
⇨ be daring=splurge

I order a lot of food and go over my budget.

(Mumblings) Budget

Today, I'll have lunch for around 600 yen.
⇨ around=about

Today, I have a budget of 900 yen.

I wanna eat something expensive once in a while.
⇨ once in a while=occasionally

I wanna go to a high class restaurant once a month.

(Mumblings) Flavor / Taste

B lunch looks delicious. / B lunch looks good.
⇨ looks delicious=looks good ; looks tasty

All the dishes look good. / All of the food looks delicious.

Which is more delicious, A or B?

This Indian curry is really good.
⇨ good=delicious; scrumptious

This is mediocre. / This tastes so so.   ⇨ so so=OK

This meat sauce is terrible. / This meat sauce sucks.   ⇨ terrible=tasteless

It was a mistake to order this food. ⇨ this food=this dish

117

こんな料理に 1,000 円も取るなんて、ひどいな。

One Point Lesson　降りる

　乗り物から「降りる」という場合は I get off at the next station.（私は次の駅で降りる）といった具合に get off を始めとして、get out、get out of などが使われます。とはいえ、これらの表現がどの乗り物についても同様に使われるわけではありません。たとえば、自転車、二輪車、馬のように私たちがまたがって乗るものについて、またバス、電車、飛行機、船など大型の乗り物については get off。しかし、乗用車、タクシー、軽飛行機といった小型の乗り物については She got out of the car.（彼女は車から降りた）といったように get out、get out of が使われます。
　ちなみに、get off の反意語「乗る」は get on。get out、get out of の反意語は get in、get into になります。また「搭乗する、乗船する、乗車する」を言い表すときは get on board。バス、電車、タクシーなどを交通機関として利用する場合は、Let's take a taxi.（タクシーに乗ろうよ）のように take とします。

One Point Lesson　ブレーキを掛ける

　「ブレーキを掛ける」は、動詞を用いた場合は He braked.（彼はブレーキを掛けた）のように brake ですが、名詞を使うと apply the brakes、または put on the brakes とします。「急ブレーキを掛ける」は slam on the brakes、slam the brakes on、jam the brakes on。「ブレーキを踏む」は step on the brakes。反対に「ブレーキを緩める」は let up on the brake、「ブレーキを外す」は take off the brake。なお、「サイドブレーキを掛ける」は ~with the parking brake on です。つまり「彼女はサイドブレーキを掛けないで駐車した」を英語に直すと She left her car with the parking brake off. となります。ちなみに「サイドブレーキ」は和製英語で、正しくは a parking brake、a hand brake といいます。

I can't believe they charge a thousand yen for this dish. / To charge a thousand yen for this food is terrible. ⇨ a thousand yen=one thousand yen ⇨ dish=food ⇨ terrible=dreadful

One Point Lesson　Go faster, man

　このような場合の man は「男」ではなく、Hey, man, don't you understand this?（よう、あんた、こいつが分からないのか）といった具合に、男女を問わず、呼びかけとして用いられることばです。なお、You are the man for this job.（君はこの仕事にうってつけの人物だ）のように、the man、the very man、one's man として「うってつけの人、おあつらえ向きの人」といった意味でも頻繁に使われます。相手の申し入れを受け入れる際に「引き受けましょう、それに乗った」などの意味合いで I'm your man. が使われるのはそのためです。

One Point Lesson　speed

　この語は人の動作や物の動きの速さを強調しており、名詞は the rate at which an object moves from one point to another を意味します。そのため、「その車は時速100キロぐらいのスピードで走っていた」は The car was moving at the speed of about 100 kilometers per hour. となります。また動詞として用いた場合は He sped the car down the street.（彼は通りを、車を飛ばして走り去った）のようになります。

　ちなみに「スピードを上げる」は pick up speed、gain speed、gather speed、動詞を使って speed up。また gas という言葉が「(車の) アクセル」を表すことから、Step on the gas.（アクセルを踏め→スピードを上げろ）という表現も頻繁に使われます。これとは反対に「スピードを落とす」は The car slowed down.（その車はスピードを落とした）といった具合に slow down、Take your foot off the gas.（アクセルから足を離せ→スピードを落とせ）などとします。なお、「猛スピード運転」「スピード違反」は speeding。

119

Chapter 3 午後

コンピュータ

描写表現　電源を入れる　　CD❶②60

コンピュータの電源を入れる。

パソコンにパスワードを入れる。

パソコンを立ち上げる。

パソコンを再起動する。

描写表現　検索

コンピュータでデータを調べる。

インターネットを閲覧する。

インターネットで情報を検索する。

アメリカ合衆国について検索する。

Google で大統領選挙を検索する。

描写表現　入力

キーボードをたたいて文字を入力する。

データを入力する。

書類をダウンロードする。

ソフトを使う

描写表現　作成　　CD❶②61

ワードで文書を作成する。

パソコンでパワーポイントを使う。

Afternoon

Computers

Descriptive expressions Turning on the computer

I turn on the computer. / I turn the computer on.

I enter my password on the computer.

I start up the computer. ⇨ start up=boot up

I restart the computer.

Descriptive expressions Search

I search for data on the computer. ⇨ data=information

I surf the Net. / I browse the Internet. ⇨ the net=the Net

I search for information on the Internet.

I search for things about the U.S.
⇨ the U.S.=the United States ; the U.S.A. ; America

I search for the Presidential election on Google.

Descriptive expressions Typing/Input

I type letters on the keyboard.

I input data.

I download documents.

Using software

Descriptive expressions Creating

I create documents using Word. ⇨ create=draw up

I use Power-point on the computer.

パワーポイントでプレゼンテーションの書類を作成する。

パワーポイントを使ってプレゼンテーションをする。

エクセルで表を作る。

エクセルでグラフを作成する。

描写表現　保存する

作成した資料を保存する。

文書をハードディスクに保存する。

データを USB メモリに保存する。

映像を DVD に保存する。

描写表現　画像処理

コンピュータで映像を編集する。

コンピュータで画像処理する。

コンピュータでお気に入りの CD を開く。

コンピュータで CD をコピーする。

描写表現　メール　　　　　　　　　　　　CD❶② 62

メールをチェックする。

添付ファイルを開く。

パソコンで手紙を書く。

アドレス帳を開く。

メールを送る。

送信先を選んでメールを送る。

I create a Power-point document for my presentation.

I make presentations using Power-point.

I make Excel tables. ⇨ tables=spreadsheets

I make graphs with Excel.

Descriptive expressions Storing/Saving

I save created data I've made. / I store created materials I've made.

I save documents on hard discs.

I store data on USB memory sticks. / I save materials on flash memory sticks.

I save movies on DVDs.

Descriptive expressions Managing pictures/ Managing graphics

I edit movies on my computer.

I manage movies on the computer. ⇨ manage=handle

I open my favorite CDs on the computer.

I copy CDs with my computer. ⇨ with=on

Descriptive expressions Mail

I check the mail.

I open attached files.

I write letters with my computer.

I open my address book. ⇨ address book=notebook

I send mail.

I select who to send the mail to. / I choose whom to send the mail to. ⇨ select=choose ⇨ the mail → my mail

取引先の会社にメールを送る。

返信メールを送る。

メールで添付ファイルを送る。

描写表現　メール SOS

メールがたまる。

メールのウイルスチェックをする。

送信先を間違える。

文書を校正しないで送る。

間違えて送信ボタンを押す。

迷惑メールを開ける。

メールが文字化けしている。

容量が大きすぎて添付ファイルが開けない。

描写表現　アプリケーション　CD❶63

コンピュータで使いたいアプリを選ぶ。

コンピュータ画面のアイコンをクリックして選ぶ。

アプリを開く。

サイトからアプリをダウンロードする。

新しいソフトを入れる。

新しいソフトをインストールする。

ソフトを立ち上げる。

ソフトをアップグレードする。

ファイルを新しいアプリで作成する。

I send mail to clients. ⇨ clients=clients' companies

I mail replies.

I attach files to the mail I send.

Descriptive expressions **Mail SOS**

The mail piles up. / My mail stacks up.

I check mail for viruses.

I make mistakes on who I send mail to.

I don't proofread documents I send.

I mistakenly hit the send button.

I open annoying mail. ⇨ annoying mail=nuisance mail; spam mail

The mail characters are gibberish. ⇨ characters=letters

The content is too large, so I can't open the mail.
⇨ too large=too much

Descriptive expressions **Apps/Applications**

I select apps to use on my computer.

I select apps by clicking on the computer screen icons. ⇨ clicking on=touching

I open applications.

I download apps from sites.

I put in new software. ⇨ put in=install

I install new software.

I run software.

I upgrade software.

I make new files with apps.

125

ソフトをインストールして不具合が生じる。

アプリをバージョンアップする。

アプリを最新のバージョンにする。

無料でソフトのバージョンアップをする。

描写表現 **アイコン**

アイコンをクリックする。

アイコンをダブルクリックする。

アイコンをドラッグする。

アイコンをドラッグしてフォルダーの上に重ねる。

画面をスクロールする。

画面をスクロールして、続きを見る。

マウスをダブルクリックする。

One Point Lesson be supposed to

I suppose he won't come.（彼は来ないと思う）のように、suppose の基本的意味が to believe something とか to assume something to be true であることから、be supposed to で to be imagined、to be expected to、to be required to などの意を表します。つまり、He is supposed to be here.（彼はここへ来ることになっている）、You are supposed to wear a seat belt in the car.（車ではシートベルトを締めることになっている）のように「～するようになっている」「～することが要求されている」の意味で使われるのです。なお、suppose が Suppose we take a coffee break.（一休みしてコーヒーを飲もう）のように、文頭に置いて命令形で用いられた場合は可能性、計画、考え、提案を示して「～してはどうか、～と仮定してみよう」といった意味を表します。この場合は Let's take a coffee break. より遠慮がちで、控えめな表現。

When I install software, I get glitches./Installing software causes glitches.

I upgrade application versions.

I do the latest application versions. ⇨ latest=newest

I upgrade versions for free.

<u>Descriptive expressions</u> **Icons**

I click icons.

I double click icons.

I drag icons.

I drag icons on top of folders.

I scroll the screen.

I scroll the screen and continue reading.

I double click the mouse.

One Point Lesson　節約する

　本書では to avoid wasting を意味する conserve を用いましたが、これ以外にも I'm going to economize this month.（今月は節約しよう）のように economize、She is economical with her money.（彼女はお金を節約している）、Be thrifty with your money.（お金を節約しなさい）、We must cut down on our use of water.（水を節約しなければいけない）、I took a taxi to save time.（時間を節約するためにタクシーを使った）などのように economize、be economical、be thrifty、cut down、save、また形式ばった表現 be frugal や curtail など、さまざまな言い方が可能です。

127

描写表現　プリンター

パソコンとプリンターを USB ケーブルで接続する。

コンピュータとプリンターを無線ランで接続する。

パソコンにプリンタードライバーをインストールする。

プリンターにインクカートリッジを入れる。

プリンターのインクカートリッジを交換する。

描写表現　その他の表現　　CD①② 64

最初の文章を削除する。

最後に 1 文章を付け加える。

書類のバックアップコピーを取る。

作成した文書をサーバーにアップロードする。

パソコンのメモリを増設する。

メモリを 1 ギガバイト増設する。

画像をパソコンに取り込む。

画像を加工処理する。

OS をアップデートする。

コンピュータを初期化する。

自分のパソコンとコンピュータをつなぐ。

OS を入れ替える。

Descriptive expressions — **Printers**

I connect my PC to the printer by USB cable.
⇨ PC=personal computer ⇨ cable=wire

I connect my computer and printer by wireless LAN. ⇨ LAN=Local Area Network

I install the printer drivers on my PC.

I put ink cartridges into my printer.

I change the printer's ink cartridges. ⇨ change=replace

Descriptive expressions — **Other expressions**

I delete the first sentence. ⇨ sentence=document

I add one sentence at the end of the documents.

I back up files. ⇨ files=documents

I upload files I've made to a server.
⇨ files=documents ⇨ a server → the server

I increase computer memory. ⇨ increase=add

I add one gigabyte to the memory. ⇨ the → my

I add graphics to my PC. / I scan a picture into the computer. / I load a picture into my computer.
⇨ to= on

I process pictures. ⇨ pictures=graphic images

I update the OS software. / I update operating system software.

I initialize the computer. ⇨ initialize=format

I connect my PC to a computer.

I change operating systems. ⇨ change=replace

ハードディスクを初期化する。

メモリを初期化する。

DVD を初期化する。

この初期化には時間がかかる。

初期化したら中身が全部消えた。

つぶやき表現　互換性

このファイルはワードで作ったんじゃないな。

このファイルは別のアプリで作成されている。

彼はこの書類をバージョンの違うアプリで作っている。

このソフトは互換性に問題がある。

このソフトは私のパソコンと互換性がない。

ワード 2000 とワード 2007 には互換性の問題がある。

つぶやき表現　コンピュータ SOS　　CD① 65

画面がフリーズした。

パソコンがウイルスに感染した。

パソコンのデータが消えた。

重要なデータの修復ができない。

わが社では私用メールは禁止だ。

このメールはすぐに削除だ。

ウエブサイトにつながらないな。

I format hard discs. ⇨ format=initialize

I format the memory.

I format DVDs.

This formatting takes time.

When I formatted, the contents disappeared.
⇨ disappeared=are deleted

Mumblings Compatibility

This file isn't made on Word, is it?

This file is made on another app. ⇨ app=application

He made this document on another application version.

This software has a compatibility problem.

This software isn't compatible with my computer.

There's a compatibility problem with Word 2000 and 2007.

Mumblings Computer SOS

The screen froze.

My computer's got a virus. / The PC's got a virus.

The PC's data is deleted. ⇨ is deleted=has been erased

I can't restore the important data.

We can't use personal mail at my company. / At our company, personal mail is not allowed.
⇨ use=do ⇨ not allowed=forbidden

I'll delete this mail right away.

I can't connect to the website.

このコンピュータは本当に遅いな。

処理速度が遅い。

データが重すぎるのかな。

コンピュータの空き容量がない。

ファイルが開けない。

A社が送ってきたファイルが開けられない。

メールサーバーがダウンした。

コンピュータのシステムに不具合が生じた。

パソコンが壊れた。

パソコンを修理してもらおう。

パソコンの使い方を教えてもらおう。

つぶやき表現　その他の表現　CD①②66

コンピュータは苦手だな。

私はアナログ人間だ。

新しい技術にはついていけないな。

長い時間キーボードを打っていたので、肩がこった。

描写表現　ブログ

ブログを始める。

ブログにコメントを書く。

ブログを更新する。

This computer is really slow.

The processing is slow.

Maybe there's too much data.

The computer doesn't have any empty space.
⇨ any empty space=any more storage space

I can't open files.

I can't open the file from A company.

The mail server went down. / The mail server is down.

The computer has developed a glitch.
⇨ developed a glitch=has a glitch

The computer is broken. ⇨ is broken=is fried

I'll get the PC fixed. / I'll have my PC repaired.

I'll get someone to teach me how to use a computer.

Mumblings Other expressions

I'm no good with computers. / I'm not good with computers.

I'm an analog person. / I'm low tech.

I can't keep up with the latest technology.
⇨ the latest=the newest

I've been using the keyboard for a long time, so I've got a stiff neck. ⇨ a stiff neck=stiff shoulders

Descriptive expressions Blogs

I've started a blog. / I've started blogging.

I write comments on blogs.

I update my blog.

133

会社で

描写表現　電話

A社の電話番号を探す。

A社に電話する。

鈴木氏の部署の内線番号を聞く。

内線234に電話をかける。

鈴木氏と電話で話す。

鈴木氏からの電話に出る。

山田氏の代わりに秘書が電話に出る。

人事部に電話を回す。

描写表現　電話の内容

友人に電話する。

電話で友人と話す。

電話で会う約束をする。

電話で彼の居場所を尋ねる。

電話で彼の明日のスケジュールを聞く。

電話で商品について尋ねる。

電話で商品の値段を聞く。

電話で店の営業時間を尋ねる。

At office

Descriptive expressions — Phone / Telephone

I look up A company's telephone number.

I call A company.

I ask for Mr. Suzuki's department extension number.

I call extension 234.

I talk to Mr. Suzuki on the phone.

I answer the phone call from Mr. Suzuki.

Mr. Yamada's secretary answers the phone instead of him.

I transfer to the human resources department.
⇨ human resources department=personnel department

Descriptive expressions — Telephone contents / Telephone details

I call friends. / I telephone my friends.

I talk to friends on the phone. ⇨ phone=telephone

I make appointments with friends on the phone.

I ask where he is on the phone.

I ask about his schedule for tomorrow on the phone. ⇨ on the phone =by phone; by telephone

I ask about products on the phone. / I enquire about merchandise on the phone.
⇨ ask about=enquire about ; inquire

I ask about product prices on the phone.
⇨ on the phone=by telephone; by phone

I ask about the store's business hours on the phone.
⇨ store's business hours=shop's business hours
⇨ business hours=operating hours

135

描写表現　伝言

伝言を残す。

鈴木氏が不在のため、秘書に伝言を残す。

私は田中氏から、鈴木氏への伝言を受ける。

私は田中氏からの伝言を、鈴木氏に伝える。

田中氏からの電話に出る。

田中氏に代わって私が電話に出る。

描写表現　その他の表現　CD① 68

電話を切る。

電話を保留にする。

相手が電話に出ない。

何度かけても相手が電話に出ない。

相手が居留守を使っている。

彼女と電話番号を交換する。

つぶやき表現　その他の表現

彼女の電話番号を知りたいな。

思い切って彼女に電話番号を聞いてみよう。

彼の部署の内線は何番だったっけ？

> Descriptive expressions   Phone messages

I leave a message.

Mr. Suzuki's out, so I leave a message with his secretary.

I get a message from Mr. Tanaka for Mr. Suzuki.
⇨ get=receive

I give the message from Mr. Tanaka to Mr. Suzuki.

I answer the phone call from Mr. Tanaka.

I answer the phone for Mr. Tanaka.

> Descriptive expressions   Other expressions

I hang up the phone.

I put the phone call on hold. / I put the phone on hold.

The other party doesn't answer the phone. / The other party isn't answering.

No matter how many times I call, the other party doesn't answer the phone.

The other party is pretending to be out. / The other party is pretending not to be in.

I exchange phone numbers with her.

> Mumblings   Other expressions

I'd really like to get her phone number. ⇨ get=learn

I'll work up the courage and ask her for her phone number.

What was his extension? / What's his extension number?

137

彼、私の電話番号を聞いてくれないかな？

彼女は電話するたびにいないんだよな。

彼女はいつ電話してもかからない。

描写表現　電話SOS

電話の声が遠い。

相手の声がよく聞こえない。

相手の声が小さすぎる。

話の途中で電話を切られる。

描写表現　携帯電話　　　　　　　　　CD② 69

携帯電話を鞄に入れる。

バッグから携帯電話を取り出す。

携帯電話のスイッチを入れる。

携帯電話で友人に電話する。

携帯電話で話す。

携帯電話が鳴る。

携帯電話をマナーモードにする。

電車に乗ると携帯電話をマナーモードにする。

友人の電話番号を携帯に入れる。

携帯電話を充電する。

I hope he'll ask me for my phone number.

Every time I call her, she's out. ⇨ she's out=she's not there

I can never get through to her.

Descriptive expressions   Telephone SOS

The voice on the phone sounds far away.

I can't hear the other party's voice very well.
⇨ other party's=other person's

The other party's voice is too soft.

I get cut off in the middle of talking.

Descriptive expressions   Cellphones/Mobile phones

I put my cellphone in my bag.

I take my cellphone out of my bag. ⇨ take=get

I turn on the switch on my cellphone. / I turn my mobile phone on.

I call my friends on my cellphone.

I talk on the cellphone.

The cellphone rings.

I set the cellphone to manner mode. ⇨ set=put

When I ride the train, I set my cellphone to manner mode. / When I get on a train, I set my mobile phone to manner mode. ⇨ set ~ to manner mode → turn off ~
⇨ manner mode=vibrate mode ; silent mode

I put my friends' numbers in my cellphone.
⇨ put=enter

I charge the cellphone. ⇨ charge=recharge

描写表現 その他の表現

携帯電話で友人にメールする。

友人から携帯電話にメールがくる。

携帯電話で写真を撮る。

携帯電話で写真を友人に送る。

写真を保存する。

写真を待ち受け画面にする。

写真をコンピュータに移す。

写真を削除する。

携帯電話を目覚まし時計として使う。

午前6時にアラームを設定する。

描写表現 スマートフォン　　　　　　　CD①70

スマートフォンでグーグル検索する。

スマートフォンで目的地の所在を調べる。

目的地に最も近いルートを調べる。

目的地までの交通費を調べる。

単語の意味を調べる。

日本語表現を英語に翻訳する。

文字が小さいので拡大する。

Descriptive expressions Other expressions

I mail my friends with my cellphone.

I get mail from my friends on the cellphone.

I take pictures with my mobile phone.

I send photos to friends on my cellphone. ⇨ photos=pix

I save the pictures.

I use the saved pictures screen. ⇨ screen=file

I transfer the pictures to my computer.
⇨ transfer=download ⇨ my computer → a computer

I delete pictures. ⇨ delete=erase

I use the cellphone as an alarm clock.

I set the alarm for six a.m. ⇨ six a.m.=six in the morning

Descriptive expressions Smartphones

I do Google searches on my smartphone. ⇨ on=with

I look up destination locations with my smartphone. ⇨ look up=check

I search for the shortest route to destinations.
⇨ search for=check for

I check the transportation costs to my destination.
⇨ transportation costs=transportation fares ; traveling expenses ; travel expenses

I look up meanings of words.

I translate Japanese expressions into English.

Letters are small, so I magnify them. / Characters are small, so I make them bigger.

画面を縮小する。

次のページに移る。

スマートフォンで YouTube を見る。

スマートフォンで映画をダウンロードする。

スマートフォンでゲームのアプリをダウンロードする。

スマートフォンで人気作家の小説を買って読む。

スマートフォンで会議の模様を録音する。

つぶやき表現　スマートフォン

この場所はスマートフォンが使えない。

電波が来てないんだな。

電波が遠いのかも知れない。

この単語をスマートフォンで調べてみよう。

このスマートフォンの容量は 16 ギガバイトだ。

容量が大きいから、かなりたくさんのゲームがダウンロードできるんだ。

メモリがいっぱいになったようだ。

この小説はコンピュータに移そう。

彼女の曲は 150 円だから安い。

描写表現　ファックス　　　　　　　　CD②71

ファックス用紙をセットする。

I shrink the screen. / I make the screen smaller.

I go to the next page. ⇨ go to=move to

I watch YouTube on my smartphone.

I download movies with my smartphone.

I download game apps with my smartphone.

I buy and read popular writers' novels with my smartphone. ⇨ writers' novels=authors' books

I record meetings with my smartphone.

> Mumblings Smartphones

I can't use a smartphone here. ⇨ I → You
⇨ here=in this place ; in this location

There's no signal.

Maybe the signal's far away. ⇨ far away=too far away

I'll look up this word on my smartphone.

This smartphone has 16 gigs of memory. / This is a 16 gigabyte smartphone. ⇨ gigs=gigabytes

The memory is large, so I can download a lot of games.

It looks like the memory is full. / It seems the memory is full.

I'll download this novel to a computer. / I'll transfer this book to my computer.

Her song is a hundred and fifty yen, so that's cheap.
⇨ song is → songs are

> Descriptive expressions Fax/Facsimile

I put in fax paper. ⇨ put in=set

ファックス番号を押す。

ファックスを送る。

田中氏からファックスを5枚受け取る。

ファックスからプリントアウトする。

ファックスに用紙を補給する。

ファックスが詰まったので、用紙を引き出す。

描写表現　**ファックスSOS**

ファックスが送れない。

ファックスが詰まる。

また送信エラーだ。

ファックスの文字がぼやけて読めない。

描写表現　**コピー**　　　　　　　　　　　　　CD❶❷ 72

コピーする。

書類をコピーする。

契約書を3部コピーする。

拡大コピーする。

縮小コピーする。

両面コピーをする。

カラーコピーをとる。

書類は文字だけだから、モノクロコピーにする。

I push the fax number. ⇨ push=enter ; hit

I send the fax.

I get a five-page fax from Mr. Tanaka. / I receive five pages of fax from Mr. Tanaka.

I print out from the fax machine.

I put paper in the fax machine. / I replenish the fax paper.

The fax machine is jammed, so I take out the paper.

> Descriptive expressions **Fax SOS**

The fax doesn't send. ⇨ send=transmit

The fax machine jams. ⇨ jams=gets stuck

Oh no, another transmission error.

The fax print is fuzzy and I can't read it. ⇨ fuzzy=obscure

> Descriptive expressions **Copy**

I copy. / I make copies.

I copy documents. ⇨ documents=paperwork

I make three copies of contracts. ⇨ contracts → the contract

I enlarge copies.

I reduce copies. / I make the copies smaller.

I copy both sides. ⇨ both sides=two sides

I make color copies.

The documents are only printed letters, so I make monochrome copies. ⇨ letters=characters
⇨ monochrome copies=black and white copies

145

コピー機に A4 の用紙を補給する。

つぶやき表現　コピーSOS

また紙詰まりだ。

誰だ、紙詰まりを起こしたのは？

ちゃんと直しとけよ。

B5 の用紙がないじゃないか。

このコピー機は作動が遅いな。

新製品に代えてほしいよ。

描写表現　コピーSOS

コピー機の調子が悪い。

コピーが遅い。

コピー機がよく詰まる。

トナーが切れている。

描写表現　郵送する

CD①② 73

指定用紙に必要事項を記入する。

書類を封筒に入れる。

書類を郵便で送る。

A 社に重要書類を書留郵便で送る。

書類を宅急便で送る。

I put A4 size paper in the copier. ⇨ copier= copy machine

Mumblings Copy SOS

The paper's jammed again. ⇨ jammed=stuck

Who caused the paper jam?

Clear it out right. / Fix it properly.

There isn't any B5 paper, is there?

This copier is slow.

I'd like them to change to a new product. / I wish we could get a new machine instead.

Descriptive expressions Copy SOS

The copier is messed up. / The copy machine's not working right.

The copies are slow.

The copier often gets jammed. / The copy machine jams up a lot.

It's out of toner. / The toner's used up.

Descriptive expressions Mailing

I write the necessary items on the designated form. ⇨ form=paper

I put the document in an envelope.

I mail the document.

I send the important document to A company by registered mail.

I send documents by express home delivery.
⇨ express home delivery=door-to-door parcel delivery ; courier service

147

手紙を普通郵便で送る。

封筒に100円切手を貼る。

郵便物に保険をかける。

描写表現　時間指定

配達時間を指定する。

配達時間を「午前中」に指定する。

One Point Lesson　小遣い

　この日本語に対応する英語表現としては pocket money、spending money、allowance があります。前者の2つはいずれもくだけた言い方で、pocket money は特に子供の小遣いを指して使われます。allowance については「特定の目的のための支給額」を意味する言葉であることから、My parents give me a ten dollars allowance a week.（両親は私に週10ドルの小遣いをくれる）のように「定期的に出る手当、こづかい」のことを言います。

描写表現　会議について　CD❶❷ 74

会議を開く。

会議の開催日を決める。

会議の開催時間を確認する。

会議の準備をする。

書類を作成する。

会議に出席する。

会議の目的について説明する。

I send letters by regular mail.

I put on a 100 yen stamp. ⇨ put= stick

I insure the mail.

> Descriptive expressions **Designating the delivery time**

I designate the delivery time. ⇨ designate=indicate ; choose

I choose "Morning delivery."

One Point Lesson　財布いろいろ

「財布」を表す一般的な英語は wallet もしくは pocketbook、それに purse。とはいえ、wallet と purse は同じものではなく、両者に少々違いがあります。たとえば wallet は billfold と同様に「札」を入れるための財布。ただし、billfold は wallet に比べて薄く、中の仕切りが少ないのです。一方、purse は留め金の付いた小銭入れ、すなわち「ガマ口」のこと。また女性用の、特に肩ひものないハンドバッグをも指して使われます。ちなみに「小銭入れ」の場合は change purse。

> Descriptive expressions **About meetings**

We open a meeting. / We call the meeting to order. ⇨ We → They → I

I decide the meeting day. / We decide the day the meeting will be held.

I confirm when the meeting will start. / I confirm what time the meeting will be held.

I prepare for the meeting.

I create documents. / I make papers.

I attend meetings.

I explain the purpose of the meeting.

出席者全員に資料を配布する。

資料について説明する。

会議にノートパソコンを持参する。

プロジェクターとパソコンを接続する。

プロジェクターを使ってプレゼンする。

会議室に USB メモリーを持参する。

描写表現　その他の表現

会議のための出席者を決める。

会議のために根回しをする。

つぶやき表現　その他の表現

この会議は長いな。

この会議は無駄だよ。

どうせ何も決まらないんだから。

あいつ、本当によくしゃべるな。

いい加減、しゃべるのはやめろよ。

この会議、早く終わってほしいよ。

今日の議題は説明しにくいな。

I hand out materials to all the attendees.
⇨ hand out=distribute

I explain the materials. ⇨ explain=explain about

I take my tablet computer to meetings.
⇨ tablet computer=notebook computer

I connect a projector to the computer. ⇨ to=and ; with

I use the projector and make presentations.

I take a USB memory chip to the meeting.
⇨ memory chip=memory stick

<u>Descriptive expressions</u>　Other expressions

I decide the meeting attendees. ⇨ decide=determine

**I talk to people in advance about the meeting. /
I pull some strings ahead of the meeting.**

<u>Mumblings</u>　Other expressions

This meeting's long, isn't it? / Boy, this is a long meeting.

This meeting is a waste of time. ⇨ a waste of time =useless

They're not going to decide anything anyway.

That guy talks a lot. / That person is really talkative.

Enough already, stop talking. / Give me a break, stop talking.

I hope this meeting ends soon. / I hope this is a short meeting.

It's hard to explain this meeting's topics for discussion. ⇨ meeting's topic for discussion=agenda

151

この出席者たちは技術者じゃないから説明するのがむずかしいよ。

この私自身も、これについてはよくわからないんだ。

ここはうまく説明しないとな。

これはうまくいきそうだな。

描写表現　企画　　　　　　　　　　　　　　CD① 75

企画を立てる。

計画書を上司に提出する。

計画の長所を説明する。

今後の方針について説明する。

会議への出席者を説得する。

計画書の不備を指摘する。

計画のデメリットについて質問する。

計画に賛成する。

計画に反対する。

部下・同僚について

つぶやき表現　性格〈肯定的〉　　　　　　　CD① 76

彼は勤勉だ。

彼はよく働く。

彼はまじめだな。

It'll be tough to explain to the attendees because they're not engineers. ⇨ tough=hard ⇨ engineers=technicians

I don't even understand this myself.

I've got to explain this very well.

It looks like this will go well. / It looks like this is gonna go well.

> Descriptive expressions **Planning / Pre-planning**

I set a plan. ⇨ set=prepare

I give the plan to my superior. ⇨ give=present
⇨ superior=boss → bosses

I explain the advantages of the plan. ⇨ advantages= strong points

I explain about the policy from now on. / I explain about the principles after this.

I persuade the attendees at the meeting. / I persuade the meeting attendees. ⇨ at=of

I point out imperfections of the plan. ⇨ point out =indicate

I ask about demerits of the plan. ⇨ demerits= disadvantages

I agree to the plan. / I approve the plan.

I disagree with the plan. / I vote against the plan.
⇨ disagree with=oppose to; object to

About subordinates and colleagues

> Mumblings **Personality<Positive>**

He's diligent. / He is industrious.

He works hard. / He is a hard worker.

He's serious, isn't he? ⇨ serious=earnest

153

彼は包容力がある。

彼は柔軟性がある。

彼は責任感が強い。

彼は人当たりがいい。

彼は社交的だ。

彼は部下からも慕われている。

彼は勇気と決断力がある。

彼は何事においても慎重だ。

つぶやき表現　　**能力〈肯定的〉**

彼はなかなか仕事ができる。

彼は仕事が早い。

彼は今の時代にマッチした人物だ。

彼は頭がキレる。

彼は物わかりがいい。

彼はセンスがある。

彼は呑み込みが早い。

彼はよく勉強している。

彼はハンサムで頭もいい。

彼はコンピュータについては実に詳しい。

この仕事は彼に任せられる。

He's broadminded. / He is tolerant.

He's flexible.

He has a strong sense of responsibility. ⇨ strong=deep

He's friendly. ⇨ friendly=affable ; charming

He's sociable.

He is loved by his men.

He has bravery and decisiveness. / He's brave and decisive. ⇨ brave=courageous

He's careful in everything. ⇨ careful=cautious ; prudent

(Mumblings) **Ability<Positive>**

He is quite an able worker.

He is a quick worker.

He's a good match for this generation.
⇨ this generation=these times

He's sharp. ⇨ sharp=smart ; clever

He is quick to understand. / He understands things well. / He grasps things readily.
⇨ quick to understand=understanding ; sensible

He's got sense. / He's sensible.

He catches on quickly./He understands quickly.

He studies a lot.

He's handsome and smart.

He's really familiar with computers. / He's very knowledgeable about computers.

He can be entrusted with this task.

例の件については彼に任せておけば大丈夫だな。

> つぶやき表現　**性格〈否定的〉**　CD❶ 77

彼は怠け者だ。

彼は横着ものだ。

彼はまったく働かない。

彼は軽率な人物だ。

彼はゴマすり野郎だ。

彼は上司の顔色ばかりうかがっている。

彼は実に無責任な男だ。

彼はほら吹きだ。

彼はうそつきだ。

> つぶやき表現　**能力〈否定的〉**

彼は頭が悪い。

彼はいつもボーッとしている。

彼は無能だ。

彼には何も任せられない。

あんな男、はやくこの会社を辞めてもらいたいよ。

> 描写表現　**他社と交渉**　CD❶ 78

顧客と会う約束をする。

顧客と会議室で会う。

If you let him take care of that matter, everything will be all right. ⇨ take care of=handle

Mumblings Personality<Negative>

He's lazy.

He's a lazybones. / He's lazy. ⇨ lazy=negligent

He doesn't work at all.

He's careless. ⇨ careless=thoughtless ; rash

He is an apple polisher. / He's a brown noser.

He always takes care not to offend his boss. / He is always sensitive to his boss's moods.

He's totally irresponsible. / He is a totally irresponsible man. ⇨ totally=completely ⇨ man=guy

He exaggerates. / He tells tall tales. / He brags.

He's a liar.

Mumblings Ability<Negative>

He's stupid. / He's thick. / He's dumb.

He's always spaced out. ⇨ spaced out=in a fog

He's good-for-nothing. / He is incompetent. / He's useless. ⇨ incompetent=an incompetent person

You can't rely on him for anything.

I want him to quit this company soon. ⇨ soon=quickly

Descriptive expressions Negotiating with other companies / firms

I promise to meet customers. ⇨ customers=clients

I meet customers in a meeting room.

A社に出かける。

部下の鈴木君を同伴する。

A社の担当者と顔を合わせる。

描写表現　**紹介**

担当者と互いに自己紹介する。

名刺を持っているか確認する。

担当者と名刺を交換する。

自分の名刺を差し出す。

相手からの名刺を受け取る。

担当者が不在だったので、自分の名刺を置いていく。

つぶやき表現　**名刺について**

しまった、名刺を忘れた。

名刺がキレそうだ。

名刺が3枚しかない。

名刺を作らないといけないな。

古い名刺を持ってきちゃった。

この名刺に書かれている役職は古いんだ。

I go to A company.

I accompany my subordinate, Mr. Suzuki. / I take my junior, Mr. Suzuki.

I meet the person in charge at A company.　⇨ at=of

Descriptive expressions Introduction

The person in charge and I introduce ourselves.

I confirm I have my business cards.

The person in charge and I exchange business cards.

I offer my business card.

I take the business card from the other person.
⇨ take=receive

The person in charge was out, so I left my business card.　⇨ was out=was not in

Mumblings About business cards

Oh no! I forgot my business cards.

I'll be out of business cards. / I'm going to run out of business cards.

I have only 3 business cards. / I only have 3 business cards.

I have to have business cards made.
⇨ have to have=have to get

I brought old business cards.

These business cards have my old position on them.　⇨ position=post

描写表現　**商談**

担当者と談笑する。

顧客に新商品の説明をする。

顧客に新商品を売り込む。

担当者と商談をする。

A社からの要望を聞く。

描写表現　**契約**

顧客と契約の交渉をする。

A社と商品の値段交渉に入る。

A社との商談をまとめる。

A社と契約を結ぶ。

A社から新商品の注文を受ける。

A社との契約を破棄する。

A社との契約が流れる。

描写表現　**報告**

上司に報告する。

上司に報告書を提出する。

上司からの指示を仰ぐ。

上司からアドバイスを受ける。

上司に今後の手続きについて尋ねる。

Descriptive expressions ▶ **Business talk**

The person in charge and I have a friendly chat.
⇨ chat=conversation

I explain new products to the client. ⇨ client=customer

I sell new products to the client. ⇨ sell=push
⇨ products=merchandise

I negotiate with the person in charge. ⇨ negotiate =bargain

I ask about A company's wishes. ⇨ wishes=desires ; demands

Descriptive expressions ▶ **Contract**

I negotiate contracts with customers.

I negotiate product prices with A company.

I reach an agreement with A company.
⇨ reach an agreement=clinch a deal

I sign contracts with A company. ⇨ sign=conclude

I receive product orders from A company.
⇨ receive=get

I cancel a contract with A company.

A contract with A company is canceled.

Descriptive expressions ▶ **Reports**

I report to seniors. ⇨ seniors=superiors ; bosses

I give written reports to my superiors. ⇨ give=present

I ask for directions from my boss. ⇨ directions= instructions

I get advice from my seniors.

I ask my superiors about what to do about follow-up procedures. ⇨ about follow-up procedures → after this

161

描写表現　クレーム　　　　　　　　　　　CD①② 80

顧客からクレームを受ける。

顧客からの要求に対応する。

商品についてA社にクレームをつける。

社員の応対についてA社にクレームをつける。

描写表現　約束SOS

約束を忘れる。

約束の時間を間違える。

約束の時間は5時だったのに、6時に指定の場所に行ってしまった。

約束の日時を間違えた。

約束の場所を間違える。

約束の時間に遅れる。

勤務

描写表現　勤務時間　　　　　　　　　　　CD①② 01

午前9時から午後5時まで勤務する。

A社で毎日8時間、勤務する。

毎朝9時から働き始める。

午後5時になると仕事を終える。

5時になるとすぐに退社する。

Descriptive expressions — Complaints

I get complaints from clients. ⇨ complaints=claims

I handle claims from customers. ⇨ handle=deal with

I complain to A company about products. / I make complaints about products to A company.

I complain to A company about the employee's manner of dealing with people. ⇨ manner=way ; style

Descriptive expressions — Promise SOS

I forget promises.

I mistake the promised time.

The promised time was 5 o'clock, but I went to the appointed place at 6 o'clock.
⇨ appointed place=designated place ⇨ place=spot

I made a mistake on the promised date.
⇨ on=about ⇨ date=day and time

I mistake the promised place.

I'm late for the promised time. ⇨ promised time=appointed time

Work

Descriptive expressions — Working hours

I work from 9 in the morning till 5 p.m. ⇨ till=until ; to

I work 8 hours every day at A company.

I start work at 9 every morning. ⇨ start work=start working

I finish work at 5 p.m.

I leave the office as soon as it's 5 o'clock. / I leave work at 5.

仕事が忙しいので、毎日、残業する。

1日3時間、残業する。

夜間勤務をする。

描写表現　**勤務成績**

仕事をこなす

まじめに仕事をする。

エネルギッシュに仕事をこなす。

勤務成績は良い。

仕事の鬼です。

仕事の虫だ。

マイペースで仕事をこなす。

いい加減に仕事をする。

さぼりながら仕事をする。

つぶやき表現　**楽しい**

仕事が楽しい。

この仕事は楽しい。

私がやりたかったのはこの仕事だ。

これは実にやりがいのある仕事だ。

つぶやき表現　**楽しくない**

仕事なんてしたくない。

この仕事はいやだ。

もうこの仕事には飽きたよ。

It's busy at work, so we work overtime every day.

I work 3 hours overtime every day.

I work the night shift. / I'm on the night shift.

Descriptive expressions Work performance

I manage work.

I work diligently. ⇨ diligently=earnestly

I manage work energetically. ⇨ manage=handle

I have shown good work performance.

I'm a fiend for work.

I'm a work addict. / I'm workaholic. / I'm a workaholic.

I do my work at my own pace.

I work half-heartedly.

I neglect my work.

Mumblings Fun

I enjoy my work.

This work is fun. ⇨ work=job

This is the job I wanted. ⇨ I wanted=I wanted to do

This is a really rewarding job. ⇨ rewarding=worthwhile

Mumblings No fun

I don't want to work. / I don't feel like working.

I don't like this job.

I'm sick and tired of this job. / I'm fed up with this work.

こんな仕事、いつでも辞めてやる。

仕事をしないで生きていける方法はないかな。

遊んで暮らせる方法なんて、ないかな。

早く誰かに養ってもらいたい。

早くいい人を見つけて結婚しよう。

親のすねでもかじろうかな。

つぶやき表現　その他の表現

連日、仕事に追われている。

やらなければいけない仕事が多くて大変だ。

まだ仕事が終わらない。

この仕事は今日の5時までに終えなければならない。

この調子だと、とても今日中には終えられない。

これだけの仕事、とても1人ではやりきれないよ。

描写表現　出張　　CD②03

出張する。

1か月に1回は出張する。

来週の月曜日に九州へ出張する。

明日、大阪支店へ出張する。

私の部署では出張が多い。

I can quit this job any time. ⇨ can quit=could quit

Isn't there a way to live without working?

Isn't there some way to live and play? ⇨ play= have fun

I want to find someone to support me. ⇨ find=get

I want to find someone soon and get married.

Maybe I'll sponge off my parents.

(Mumblings) Other expressions

Day after day I'm pressed by work. / Work is hectic every day.

I have so much work I have to do. / I have so much work that must be done that it's killing me.

The work's still not done. ⇨ still not done=still unfinished

I have to finish this job by 5 o'clock today.

At this rate, I can't finish this job today.
⇨ at this rate=the way it's going

I can't do this work by myself. / One person can't handle this job.

(Descriptive expressions) Business trip

I go on business trips. / I take business trips.

I travel on business once a month.

I'm going on a business trip to Kyushu next Monday.

I'm taking a business trip to a branch office in Osaka tomorrow.

My section has a lot of business trips. ⇨ section= department

167

仕事の関係で、関西への出張が多い。

私の部署では全く出張がない。

私は一度も出張したことがない。

つぶやき表現　　**出張**

出張が多くて嫌になる。

1週間のうち、自宅で過ごすのは2日だけだ。

やれやれ、明日もまた札幌へ出張だ。

九州の工場へ日帰りで出張だなんて、疲れるよな。

明日から、1週間ほど海外へ出張だ。

たまには私も大阪支社へ出張したいな。

描写表現　　**休憩時間**　　　　　　　　　　　CD①②04

休憩する。

仕事の合間に休憩する。

1時間のうち10分間、休憩する。

午前中に20分ほど休憩する。

午後3時に30分間コーヒーブレイクを取る。

仕事の能率を上げるために、疲れた時には休憩する。

休憩は取らない。

午前中は休憩を取らない。

I take a lot of business-related trips to Kansai.

My section doesn't take business trips at all.

I've never taken a business trip.

> Mumblings Business trip

I hate taking a lot of business trips.

I stay at home only 2 days a week.

Oh no! I have to go on a business trip to Sapporo again tomorrow.

I'm gonna be tired on a one day return trip to a factory in Kyushu. ⇨ factory=plant

I'm going on a business trip overseas for about a week from tomorrow.

I want to take a business trip to the Osaka branch office now and then, too.
⇨ I want to=I'd like to ⇨ now and then=occasionally

> Descriptive expressions Break time/Between jobs

I take a break.

I take a break between jobs.

I take a 10-minute break an hour.

I take about a 20-minute break in the morning.

I take a 30-minute coffee break at 3 o'clock.

I take a break when I'm tired to improve work efficiency.

I don't take breaks.

I don't take a break in the morning.

周りの人がみんな熱心に仕事をしているので、私も休憩は取らない。

つぶやき表現　休憩時間

休憩が欲しいな。

早く休憩がしたいな。

うちのボスは私たちが休憩を取ると、いい顔しないんだよな。

疲れたよ、もう3時間も働きづくめだ。

ずっと座っているので、腰が痛い。

何時間もコンピュータを使っているので、肩がこる。

毎日、コンピュータ画面の小さな文字ばかり見ているので、目が疲れる。

私は立ち仕事なので、足がだるい。

接客業なので、神経が疲れる。

しゃべる仕事なので、喉が痛い。

肉体労働なので、体中が痛い。

描写表現　給料　CD①②05

給料をもらう。

Everyone around is working earnestly, so I won't take a break. ⇨ earnestly=enthusiastically

> Mumblings **Break time/Between jobs**

I wanna take a break. ⇨ wanna=want to

I wanna take a break soon. ⇨ soon=early

If we take a break the boss looks displeased.
⇨ displeased=unhappy

I'm tired; I've been working hard for three hours.

I've been sitting down a long time, so my back aches. ⇨ my back aches=my lower back hurts

I've been using a computer for hours, so my shoulders are stiff.
⇨ my shoulders are stiff → my neck is stiff

I look at small letters every day on the computer screen, so my eyes are tired.
⇨ letters=characters ⇨ my eyes are tired → I've got dry eyes

I work standing up, so my legs are tired.
⇨ standing up=standing on my feet

It's a service industry, so my nerves are shot.
⇨ shot=frazzled

I talk in my job, so my throat hurts.

It's manual labor, so my whole body hurts.
⇨ manual labor=physical labor ⇨ hurts=aches

> Descriptive expressions **Pay**

I get paid. / I receive my salary.

毎月、月末に給料をもらう。

今日、今月の給料を受け取る。

給料が銀行の口座に振り込まれる。

給料の明細を受け取る。

銀行に振り込まれた今月の給料の額を見て、ショックを受ける。

描写表現　**給料日**

今日は給料日なので同僚と飲みに行く。

今日はみんなで酒を飲んで大騒ぎをする。

臨時ボーナスが入ったので、みんなにおごる。

同僚と1人1,000円で飲み放題、食べ放題の店へ行く。

夜遅くまでどんちゃん騒ぎをする。

給料が少ないので、友人たちとお茶で乾杯する。

描写表現　**安い**

私の給料は安い。

I get paid at the end of the month.
⇨ at the end of the month= at the end of every month

I get paid for this month today. / I receive this month's pay today.

My pay is transferred to my bank account.
⇨ is transferred → is automatically transferred

I get the statement of my pay. ⇨ statement=detail

I get shocked when I see the pay transferred to my bank account this month.
⇨ see=look at
⇨ pay=wages

Descriptive expressions ▶ **Payday**

Today's payday, so I'll go drinking with my colleagues. ⇨ colleagues=co-workers

Today, I'll have a great time drinking with my friends. / Today, I'll make merry drinking with everyone.

I got a special bonus, so I'll treat everyone.
⇨ special=extra

I'll go with my colleagues to a shop that's 1,000 yen per person for all you can eat and drink.
⇨ colleagues=co-workers ⇨ shop=place

We'll party till late at night. / We'll have a hearty blowout till late at night.

My salary is not very much, so I'll have a toast of tea with some friends. ⇨ My salary is not very much=
My pay is very little

Descriptive expressions ▶ **Cheap / inexpensive / low**

My salary's low.

173

私の給料は鈴木君より3万円ほど安い。

私の1か月の給料はわずか25万円だ。

私たちの業界は給料が安い。

描写表現　**高い**

わが社は給料が高いので有名だ。

私の給料は同じ年齢の全国平均より5万円も高い。

私の給料は高いほうだと思う。

私の給料は大学の同級生たちと比べて、4万円高い。

私は25歳で、年収はだいたい1千万円だ。

描写表現　**平均的**

私の給料は全国平均だ。

私の年齢の平均的な給料は1か月30万円前後だ。

わが社の給料は高くも安くもない。

描写表現　**ボーナス**

ボーナスは年に2回出る。

My salary is 30 thousand yen lower than Mr. Suzuki's.

I only make 250,000 yen a month. / My pay is a mere 250 thousand yen a month.

Our industry has low pay. / Our industry is low paying.

Descriptive expressions — High / Expensive

Our company is famous for high pay.
⇨ famous=well-known   ⇨ pay=salaries

My pay is fifty thousand yen higher than the national average for people of the same age.
⇨ pay=salary   ⇨ higher=more

I think my pay's on the high side. / I believe my pay is rather high.

My salary is 40 thousand yen a month higher than my university classmates'.
⇨ than my=compared to my

I'm twenty-five and make around ten million yen a year. / I'm 25 years old and earn about 10 million yen a year.   ⇨ make=earn   ⇨ around=about

Descriptive expressions — On average/average

My salary is the national average.

The salary for people of my age is around three hundred thousand yen a month

Our company's pay isn't high or low.

Descriptive expressions — Bonus

I get a bonus twice a year.

夏のボーナスは1か月の給料の1.5倍だ。

冬のボーナスは1か月の給料の2倍だ。

わが社は能力主義なので、成果を上げた人にはボーナスがどっさり出る。

不景気なので、わが社ではボーナスが出ない。

昨年はボーナスが出たが、今年は出ない。

つぶやき表現　その他の表現

給料、安すぎるよ。

こんなに働いて、1か月たった15万円か。

もっと給料が欲しいよ。

給料を上げてくれないかな。

ボーナスが出ないなんて、信じられない。

他の会社ではボーナスが月給の3倍だってのにさ。

年収がこんなに少ないと結婚もできないよ。

この金額じゃあ、家族を養ってなんかいけない。

描写表現　昇給

わが社では年に1度、昇給がある。

わが社は年齢給だ。

The summer bonus is one point five times our monthly salary. ⇨ salary=pay

The winter bonus is twice our monthly salary.
⇨ salary=pay ; wages

My company's performance based, so people with good results get huge bonuses. ⇨ huge bonuses =big bonuses

Due to the poor economy, our company doesn't pay bonuses. ⇨ poor economy=recession
⇨ pay bonuses=give bonuses

I got a bonus last year, but not this year.

> Mumblings Other expressions

The pay's too low. / My salary's too low.

I get only a hundred and fifty thousand yen a month for all of this work. ⇨ for all of this work=for this work ; for working so hard

I want more money. ⇨ money=salary ; pay

I wonder if they'll raise my pay. ⇨ raise my pay= increase my salary

I can't believe I don't get a bonus. / I can't believe we won't get a bonus.

Heck, other companies pay a bonus of three months' pay. ⇨ pay=give

With an annual income this low, I can't get married.

I can't support a family with this amount of money.

> Descriptive expressions Raise / Pay raise

We get a raise once a year. ⇨ raise=pay increase

We get paid based on age. ⇨ age=seniority

1歳年を取るごとに2,000円給料が上がる。

わが社は能力給だ。

業績を上げなければ給料は上がらない。

今年は1か月の給料の1.8%の昇給がある。

描写表現　**休暇**

わが社は休みが多い。

わが社では誰もが1年に1か月間、休暇を取ることができる。

わが社では年に40日ほど休みがある。

わが社は休みが少ない。

わが社では休みが全く取れない。

わが社では休みが取りづらい。

誰も休暇を取らないから、私も取りにくい。

休みを取ると、昇進に影響しそうだ。

つぶやき表現　**休暇**

休みを取りたいな。

来週は休みを取ろう。

We get a two thousand yen salary increase for every year we get older.

Our company pays based on performance.
⇨ performance=ability

If we don't get results, we don't get a raise. / If we don't achieve, we don't get a salary increase.

This year we get a one point eight percent monthly raise.

Descriptive expressions Vacation/Paid vacation

Our company has a lot of days off.

At our company, everyone can take a one-month vacation a year. ⇨ everyone=everybody

At our company, we get about 40 days off a year. ⇨ off=vacation

At our company, we don't have many days off.

At our company, we can't take a vacation at all.
⇨ take a vacation=take days off

It's hard to take days off at our company.
⇨ hard=difficult

Nobody takes a vacation, so it's hard for me to take a day off.

It seems that if you take days off, you don't get promoted. / It seems that if you take vacations, you don't advance.

Mumblings Vacation/Paid vacation

I wanna take a day off. ⇨ take a day off=take a vacation

I'll take a day off next week.

今度の夏は 2 週間ほど休みを取ろう。

休みをとって家庭サービスをしよう。

この正月は休みを取って、友人と 1 週間ほどハワイへ行こうかな。

来月の連休には子供たちをディズニーランドへ連れて行こう。

たまの休みぐらい 1 日中のんびり家で過ごしたい。

One Point Lesson　papers と document

　紙に書かれたり、印刷された書類は、通例、papers といった具合に複数形で表します。ここから、「公文書」は state papers、「印刷物」は printed papers となります。また、「書類に署名する」は sign papers。なお、document とした場合は export documents（輸出書類）、a democratic document（外交文書）といった具合に正式な書類、文書のことで、少々堅苦しい言い方。

One Point Lesson　給料

　「給料」を表す英語に pay、wage、salary がありますが、pay が最も一般的な語で、あらゆる種類の給料について用いられます。一方 wage、wages は an hourly wage（時間給）、weekly wages（週給）のように、単純労働や肉体労働に対して 1 時間、1 日、1 週間を単位として支給される「賃金、給金」。salary の場合は公務員、会社員など比較的高い技術を持つ人、また地位の高い人物に対して定期的に固定給として支払われる a monthly salary（月給）、an annual salary（年棒）のこと。その他、余り一般的ではないが、stipend という言葉があります。これは専門知識、特殊技能に対する報酬、固定給を指し、イギリスでは、通例、牧師、教授、裁判官などの給料について用いられています。

I'll take about a two-week vacation this summer.

I'll take a vacation and work at home. / I'll take some time off and do household chores.
⇨ work at home → play the good family man

Maybe I'll take a week's vacation at New Year's and go to Hawaii with a friend.
⇨ with a friend → with friends

Next month's consecutive days off, I'll take the kids to Disneyland.
⇨ days off=vacation
⇨ the kids=my children

Sometimes I just wanna stay home all day on my day off and relax at home.

One Point Lesson　「理由」について

　Give me the reason you were late.（遅れた理由を言いなさい）のように、reason はある事態の由来についての論理的説明を表す言葉です。類似したものに cause がありますが、これは What was the cause of the traffic accident?（その交通事故の原因は何ですか）のように、ある結果を必然的にもたらす原因のこと。ground は That will give you every ground for divorce.（それはあなたにとって離婚の十分な理由になる）のように、本人が正当性を信じて主張する理由、根拠。motive は He did it from personal motives.（彼はそれを個人的な動機で行なった）のように、ある行動に駆り立てる動機また要因。occasion は What's the occasion for this riot?（この暴動の原因は何ですか）のように、ある事態を引き起こすきっかけ。excuse は He made a poor excuse for being late.（彼は遅刻の下手な言い訳をした）のように、不都合な行為などに対して非難や処罰を避けようとして使う言い訳、口実。pretext は真の意図を隠すための偽りの理由のことで、excuse の少し堅い表現。

学校で

描写表現　授業中

まじめに授業を受ける。

教師の説明に耳を傾ける。

講義のメモを取る。

教師が黒板に書いたことをノートに書き写す。

講義の一部を聞き逃す。

講義が理解できない。

途中で講義に飽きてくる。

授業中、眠くなる。

つぶやき表現　授業中

この授業は面白いな。

これは本当にためになる。

この講義は将来、役に立ちそうだ。

先生の話、ほとんど理解できない。

先生が何言ってるのか全然わからないよ。

この先生、説明の仕方が下手なんだ。

先生の声が小さくて、よく聞こえない。

先生の言葉は難しすぎるよ。

内容が難しくて、わからない。

At school

Descriptive expressions — During class

I take lessons seriously. / I'm serious in class.

I listen to the teacher's explanations.

I take notes of lectures.

I take note of what the teacher writes on the blackboard. ⇨ writes=puts

I miss hearing a part of the lecture.

I can't understand the lecture. ⇨ I can't=I don't

I get tired during the lecture.

I get sleepy during lectures.

Mumblings — During class

This lecture is interesting.

This is really useful. ⇨ useful=profitable ; beneficial

I think this lecture will be useful in the future.

I can't understand most of what the teacher says.

I don't understand at all what the teacher is saying.

This teacher is poor at explaining things. / This teacher is bad at explanations.

The teacher has a soft voice, so I can't hear well.

The teacher's words are too difficult.
⇨ words are=vocabulary is

The content is difficult, so I don't understand.

先生の話はつまらない。

この授業、退屈だな。

先生の話し方が単調すぎて、眠くなる。

この授業、早く終わってくれないかな。

描写表現　授業終了

授業終了まであと5分。

授業が終わるのが待ち遠しい。

授業が終わる。

授業終了のベルが鳴る。

席を立つ。

教室を出る。

つぶやき表現　その他の表現

今度は好きな授業だ。

次の授業は面白い。

社会は私の最も得意な科目だ。

あらゆる科目の中でこれが一番好きだ。

3限目は私の苦手な科目だ。

文学の先生は面白い。

一郎先生は楽しいから好きだ。

The teacher's talks are boring.

This class is boring.

The teacher's way of speaking is too monotonous, and I get sleepy.

I wish this class would end soon. / I hope this class ends quickly.

Descriptive expressions End of class

It's five minutes till the class ends. / It's 5 minutes until the lesson finishes.

I'm eagerly waiting for the class to end. ⇨ eagerly= anxiously

The class is over.

The bell rings to end the lesson.

I get up. / I get up from my seat.

I leave the classroom.

Mumblings Other expressions

Next is a class I like. ⇨ a class=the class

The next class is interesting.

Social studies is my best subject.

This is my favorite of all the subjects.

The third period class is not a subject I'm good at. / I'm not good at the third period class subject.

Our literature teacher is interesting. ⇨ Our=The

Teacher Ichiro is fun, so I like him.

一郎先生はわかりやすく説明してくれるから好きだ。

授業中

描写表現　**質問**　　　　　　　　　　　　　　　CD①②11

先生が質問をする。

私は先生の質問に答える。

私は手を挙げて質問する。

先生が私をあてる。

私は当てられないように下を向く。

授業中、私は先生の目を見ないようにする。

間違った答えを言う。

トンチンカンな答えをしてクラスメートに笑われる。

質問の答えがわからないので黙っている。

つぶやき表現　**質問**

質問の意味がわからないよ。

質問の答えがわからない。

先生の質問にどう答えてよいかわからない。

そんな質問するなって。

私をあてないで。

I like teacher Ichiro because his explanations are easy to understand.

During class

Descriptive expressions Questions

The teacher asks questions.

I answer the teacher's questions.

I raise my hand and ask questions.

The teacher calls on me.

I look down to avoid being called on.
⇨ being called on=being picked

I avoid eye-contact with the teacher. / I avoid looking into the teacher's eyes.

I give the wrong answer. / I answer incorrectly.

I give an absurd answer and my classmates laugh at me.

I don't know the answer to the question, so I keep quiet.

Mumblings Questions

I don't understand the meaning of the question. / I don't know what the question means.

I don't know the answer to the question.

I don't know how to answer the teacher's question.

Don't ask such a question. / Don't ask me a question like that.

Don't call on me.

この先生、よく私を当てるんだから。

もう私には質問しないでほしいよ。

まずい、先生と目があっちゃった。

当てられるぞ。

当てられなくてよかった。

やさしい質問で助かった。

答えがあっててよかった。

描写表現　ノート　CD①②12

授業の内容をまとめる。

級友からノートを借りる。

級友にノートを貸してくれと頼まれる。

先生が黒板に書いたことを書き写す。

先生の説明を聞き逃す。

描写表現　授業中のおしゃべり

授業中、隣の人とおしゃべりをする。

隣の人としゃべっていて、先生に注意される。

横の生徒がおしゃべりをしているので腹が立つ。

周りの生徒たちがおしゃべりを止めないので、集中できない。

This teacher calls on me a lot.

Don't ask me anymore questions.

Oh no, I caught the teacher's eye.

I'm gonna be called on. ⇨ be called on=be picked

I'm glad I wasn't called on.

I'm glad it was an easy question.

I'm glad the answer was right. ⇨ right=correct

Descriptive expressions Notes

I summarize the details of the lesson.
⇨ details=contents

I borrow a classmate's notes. / I borrow notes from a classmate.

A classmate asks to borrow my notes. / A classmate asks me to lend him my notes.
⇨ to lend him → to lend her

I write down what the teacher wrote on the blackboard. ⇨ write down=copy

I miss hearing the teacher's explanation.

Descriptive expressions Talking during class

During class, I talk to the student next to me.

The teacher warns me for talking to the student next to me.

I get upset because the student beside me talks a lot.

The students around me won't stop talking, so I can't concentrate. ⇨ won't stop talking → don't stop talking

189

つぶやき表現　授業中のおしゃべり

この連中、うるさいんだよ。

なんで田中先生はおしゃべりしている人たちを注意しないんだ。

この人たちをしかってくださいよ。

こんな人が教師をやっているからダメなんだ。

この生徒たち、授業中だってことを忘れてるんじゃないの。

描写表現　試験　CD①②13

来週は試験です。

来週の月曜日から土曜日まで1週間は試験期間です。

今週は3科目試験がある。

明日から期末テストが始まる。

中間試験が今週の水曜日から来週の火曜日まで行なわれる。

試験を受ける。

良い成績を取る。

英語の試験で満点を取る。

試験の結果は上々だ。

試験の結果は散々だ。

この試験では70%はできたと思う。

全ての質問に答えることができた。

Mumblings Talking during class

These people are noisy.

Why doesn't Ms. Tanaka warn the people who are talking? ⇨ Ms. Tanaka → Mr. Tanaka

Please scold these people.

People like this are teachers, so that's bad.
⇨ bad= no good

These students seem to forget we're in the middle of class.

Descriptive expressions Exams/Tests

Next week is the test. / We have exams next week.

Next week from Monday through Saturday we have a week of tests.

I have three tests this week.

End of term tests start next week. / Final exams begin next week.

Mid-term exams are from this Wednesday through next Tuesday.

I take tests.

I get a good score./I get good results.
⇨ good score=good result; high mark

I get a perfect score on the English exam.

I got a good score on the exam. ⇨ good score= good result

My test results were terrible. ⇨ terrible=dreadful

I think I got 70% on this test.

I could answer all of the questions. ⇨ could answer= answered

最後の質問はわからなかった。

どの質問も全くわからなかった。

つぶやき表現　試験　　　　　　　　　　　　　　CD①②14

明日から試験だ。

試験なんて大嫌いだ。

田中先生はいつも試験をする。

試験をすればいいってもんじゃないよ。

今度の試験は頑張らないといけないな。

特に英語の試験は頑張らないとね。

前回の試験は散々だったから。

今学期はオールAを目指すぞ。

クラスで1番を取ろう。

試験の準備はしっかりできているよ。

描写表現　その他の表現

机の物をすべて引き出しに入れる。

机の上には筆記用具だけ出す。

携帯電話は電源を切って、鞄に入れる。

試験のとき、辞書の参照不可。

描写表現　宿題　　　　　　　　　　　　　　CD①②15

数学の先生が宿題を出す。

I didn't understand the last question.

I didn't understand any of the questions.

Mumblings Exams/Tests

We have tests from tomorrow.

I hate tests.

Ms. Tanaka always has tests. / Mr. Tanaka always gives tests.   ⇨ Ms. → Miss → Mr.

If you think giving tests is a good thing, you're mistaken.

I have to try hard on the next test.

I especially have to try hard on the English exam.

My last test was terrible.

I'm gonna aim for all As this term.   ⇨ aim for=try for

I'll get the best score in the class.   ⇨ best=top

I'm completely prepared for the test.

Descriptive expressions Other expressions

I put everything on my desk in the drawer.

I take out only my pencil box and put it on the desk.

I turn off my cellphone and put it in my bag.
⇨ cellphone=mobile phone

We can't use dictionaries during the test.

Descriptive expressions Homework

Our math teacher gives homework.   ⇨ gives=assigns

理科の教師は毎週、難しい宿題を出す。

宿題がある。

今日は英語の宿題がどっさりある。

毎日、いろんな科目の宿題が出る。

田中先生は宿題を出さない。

世界史の先生は宿題を出さないから好きだ。

宿題の提出日は明日だ。

宿題の提出日までもう3日しかない。

まだ数学の宿題が終わっていない。

アメリカ文化についてのレポートを書く。

友人のレポートをまる写しする。

宿題をやる。

友だちと一緒に宿題をする。

宿題のために図書館へ行く。

社会の宿題をするためにインターネットで調べる。

宿題をやらない。

宿題をするのを忘れる。

宿題を提出する。

The science teacher gives difficult homework every week. ⇨ gives=assigns

I have homework.

I've got a lot of English homework. ⇨ a lot of= oodles of

We get homework in many subjects every day.

Ms. Tanaka doesn't assign homework.
⇨ Ms. Tanaka → Mr. Tanaka ⇨ assign=give

The World History teacher doesn't give homework, so I like her. ⇨ her → him

The deadline for homework is tomorrow. / I have to turn in my homework tomorrow.

I have only three more days to hand in homework. / We only have three more days to turn in our homework.

I haven't finished my math homework yet.

I write a report about American culture.

I completely copy my friend's report.

I do homework.

I do homework with a friend. ⇨ a friend → friends

I go to the library to do homework.

I look up things on the Internet for social studies homework. ⇨ look up things=search

I don't do homework.

I forget to do my homework.

I hand in my homework. ⇨ hand in= turn in

つぶやき表現　宿題

宿題は嫌だな。

宿題はやりたくない。

毎日、宿題があるので嫌になる。

あの教師は、宿題を出すのが趣味だからな。

宿題が出るたびに、英語が嫌いになる。

宿題のない世界へ行きたいよ。

描写表現　その他の表現

鉛筆で書く。

ボールペンを使う。

黒板の文字をノートに書き写す。

間違えた答えを消しゴムで消す。

鉛筆のシンを鉛筆削りでとがらす。

文字を書くとき下敷きを使う。

One Point Lesson　seat について

　seat とは乗り物、劇場などの固定された座席のこと。そこから「窓側の席」は a window seat、「通路側の席」は an aisle seat、「後部座席」は a back seat、「前の座席」は a front seat、「座席指定」は a reserved seat ticket、「上座」は a seat of honor、「座席を予約する」は reserve a seat、「空席を見つける」は find a vacant seat、find an empty seat、「起立する」は rise from one's seat、「席に着いたままでいてください」は Keep your seat、Hold your seat、「もっといい席に替えたい」は I want to change my seat for a better one. とします。また、「私はバスの中で老人に席を譲った」は I gave my seat on the bus to an old person.、「この席、空いてますか」は Is this seat vacant? とか Is this seat free? とすればよいでしょう。なお、「ふさがっています」は It's taken. あるいは It's occupied.「この席を取っておいて」は Will you save this seat for me?、Can you keep this seat for me? です。

Mumblings Homework

I hate homework.

I don't wanna do homework.

I hate having homework every day. / I get fed up with homework every day.

That teacher likes giving homework. / That teacher's hobby is assigning homework.

Every time I have homework, I hate English.

I wanna go to a place without homework. ⇨ place =world

Descriptive expressions Other expressions

I write with a pencil.

I use a ballpoint pen.

I copy the letters written on the blackboard.

I erase wrong answers with an eraser.

I sharpen the pencil with a pencil sharpener.

I use a desk pad when I write letters.
⇨ letters=characters

One Point Lesson ゴミ

　ゴミは種類によって、またイギリス英語とアメリカ英語で言い方が異なります。紙、木片、ぼろ布、ビンなどのゴミはアメリカでは trash、イギリスでは rubbish、格式ばった言葉は refuse。また道路などに散らかっているゴミは litter、くず入れは a litter receptacle、台所の生ごみはアメリカでは garbage、イギリスでは rubbish。廃棄物は waste、産業廃棄物は industrial waste。

　ちなみに「ゴミ箱」はアメリカでは trash can、「台所のゴミ入れ」は garbage can、イギリスではどちらも dustbin。「くずかご」はアメリカでは wastepaper basket、wastebasket、イギリスでは waste bin。また「ゴミ収集車」はアメリカでは garbage truck、イギリスでは dustcart、「ゴミ収集人」はアメリカでは garbage man、garbage collector、sanitation engineer、イギリスでは dustman となります。

| 描写表現 | 散歩

家の近くを散歩する。

健康のために毎朝、30分ほど散歩する。

帰宅するとすぐに愛犬を連れて散歩に出かける。

| 描写表現 | **その他の表現**

彼氏とコンサートへ行く。

AKAたちの歌に合わせて手拍子する。

彼と富士五湖へドライブに行く。

サイクリングに行く。

サッカーの試合を見に行く。

浦和イエローを応援する。

近くの公園へ花見に出かける。

秋の紅葉を楽しむために大雪山に登る。

自然を楽しむために田舎へ行く。

渋谷で女の子をナンパする。

A社の女の子たちと合コンする。

休日はボランティア活動をする。

Descriptive expressions **Taking a walk**

I take a walk in my neighborhood.

I walk 30 minutes every morning for my health.
⇨ for my health=for health

As soon as I get home, I take the dog out for a walk. / As soon as I get home, I go out to walk the dog.

Descriptive expressions **Other expressions**

I go to a concert with him. ⇨ with him=with my boyfriend

I clap hands to AKA's songs.

I go for a ride with him to the Fuji five lakes.
⇨ with him=with my boyfriend

I go cycling.

I go to a soccer game. ⇨ soccer game=football match

I root for Urawa Yellow. ⇨ root for=cheer for

I go out to see the cherry blossoms in a nearby park. ⇨ go out to see the cherry blossoms=go cherry blossoms viewing

I climb Mount Daisetsu to enjoy the fall colors.
⇨ fall colors=autumn leaves

I go to the country to enjoy nature. ⇨ country=rural areas

I hit on a girl in Shibuya. / I try to pick up girls in Shibuya.

I mix with girls from A company. / We have a singles party with A company's women. ⇨ girls=ladies

I do volunteer work on days off. ⇨ work=activities

199

連休を利用して東北地方へボランティア活動に行く。

農場で野菜の収穫をする。

描写表現　計画　　　　　　　　　　　　　CD①②18

旅行の計画を立てる。

将来の計画を立てる。

明日の予定を立てる。

今度の土曜日のデートの計画を立てる。

描写表現　デートする

彼女に電話する。

彼女をデートに誘う。

彼女を映画に誘う。

待ち合わせ場所を決める。

待ち合わせ時間を決める。

彼女と駅前で待ち合わせをする。

約束の時間より少し早めに待ち合わせ場所へ行く。

待ち合わせ場所で彼女を10分待つ。

映画館の入口で彼女を待つ。

I go to the Tohoku region on vacation to do volunteer work. / I use vacation time to perform volunteer activities in the Tohoku region.
⇨ Tohoku → the northeast   ⇨ on vacation=on holidays

I harvest vegetables on a farm.

Descriptive expressions — Plans

I plan a trip. / I make travel plans.

I make a plan for the future. / I plan for the future.

I make tomorrow's schedule. ⇨ schedule=plan

I plan for next Saturday's date.

Descriptive expressions — Dating

I call my girlfriend.

I invite her for a date. ⇨ invite=ask

I invite her to a movie.

I decide on a meeting place. / I decide where to meet.

I decide time to meet. / I decide when to meet.

I meet her at the front of the station. / I meet her in front of the train station.

I go to the meeting place a bit earlier than arranged. ⇨ a bit earlier=a little early

I wait for her ten minutes at the meeting place.

I wait for her at the movie theater entrance.
⇨ movie theater=movie theatre ; movie-hall ; cinema

彼女を家まで迎えに行く。

描写表現　チケット　　　　　　　　　　　　　　CD①②19

チケットを買う。

二人分のチケットを買う。

家族全員の入場券を買う。

チケットを買うために列に並ぶ。

列の最後尾に立つ。

30分並んで、やっとチケットを手に入れる。

ネットでチケットを予約する。

つぶやき表現　チケット

たくさん人が並んでいるな。

長い列だな。

これじゃチケットを買うだけで1時間もかかっちゃうよ。

もっと早くしてくれないかな。

あの男性、割り込みをしようとしている。

描写表現　写真

記念写真を撮る。

彼女の写真を撮る。

I go to meet her at her house. / I go to her place to pick her up.

Descriptive expressions Ticket

I pay for a ticket. ⇨ pay for=pay

I pay for two people. ⇨ for two people=for two

I pay the entrance charge for all the family.
⇨ charge=fee ⇨ for all the family=for the whole family

I stand in line to buy tickets. ⇨ stand in line=queue up
⇨ to buy tickets=to pay for tickets

I stand at the end of the line. ⇨ stand=line up

After standing in line for 30 minutes, I get tickets.

I reserve tickets on-line. ⇨ on-line=on the net ; on the Net

Mumblings Ticket

A lot of people are in line. / There are a bunch of people lined up.

It's a long line.

The way it is, it'll take an hour to get a ticket.
⇨ an hour=one hour ⇨ to get=to buy ⇨ a ticket → tickets

Won't they hurry up? ⇨ hurry up=go faster

That man's trying to cut in line. / That guy's thinking of cutting in line.

Descriptive expressions Photographs / Photos / Pictures / Pix

I photograph a memorial picture. / I take a memorial photo.

I take my girlfriend's picture. ⇨ picture=photo

パンダを背景に彼女の写真を撮る。

近くにいた人に私たちの写真を撮ってもらう。

つぶやき表現　デート　　　　　　　　　CD①②20

明日は彼女と初めてのデートだ。

待ちきれないよ。

早く明日が来ないかな。

デートには何を着て行こうかな？

久しぶりのデートだからおしゃれをしよう。

どんな映画を観ようかな？

今、どんな映画をやっているのかインターネットでチェックしてみよう。

どこか、ロマンティックな映画をやっているところはないかな？

彼女、どんな映画が好きだったっけ？

描写表現　愛の告白　　　　　　　　　CD①②21

彼女に愛を告白する。

彼女に自分の気持ちを伝える。

彼女に交際を申し込む。

彼女に指輪を差し出す。

I take a photo of her with a panda in the background. ⇨ take a photo=take a shot

I have a photo of us taken by a nearby person. / I get our picture taken by a person beside us.

(Mumblings) Date

Tomorrow's my first date with her. / Tomorrow's our first date.

I can't wait.

Why can't tomorrow be here? ⇨ be here=come soon

What should I wear for our date? / What shall I wear on the date?

I haven't dated in a while, so I'll dress up.
⇨ in a while=in a long time

What movie should we watch? ⇨ What movie= What kind of movie

I'll see what movies are showing now on the Internet. ⇨ see=check ⇨ are showing=are being shown

Isn't there any theater showing romances now? / What theaters are showing romances now?

What kind of movies does she like? / What kind of movies is it my girlfriend gets into?

(Descriptive expressions) Confessing love

I confess my love to her. / I profess my love to my girlfriend.

I tell her how I feel.

I ask her to date. ⇨ date=hang out

I give her a ring.

205

彼女の手を握る

彼女と手をつなぐ。

彼女に体に腕を回す。

彼女にキスをする。

彼を受け入れる。

彼を拒絶する。

返事をしない。

考える時間が欲しいと彼に伝える。

彼の手を振り払う。

彼の手を握り返す。

つぶやき表現　その他の表現

彼、今日はキマッてるわね。

彼ったら、今日はホットだわ。

彼女、いつもと違うぞ。

今日はすごく輝いて見える。

彼女に惚れ直したよ。

最近はデートがマンネリ化してきたな。

デートするたびに、口げんかだ。

何をしても面白くない。

I grasp her hand. / I hold her hand.

I hold hands with her.

I put my arms around her. ⇨ around her=around her body

I kiss her.

I accept him.

I refuse him. / I decline him.

I don't answer. ⇨ answer=respond

I tell him I want to think about it. / I tell him I'll think it over.

I shake off his hand. / I whisk off his hand.
⇨ shake off=brush off

I grab his hand in return. / I hold his hand in return.

Mumblings Other expressions

He looks pretty sharp today. ⇨ sharp=cool

He's hot today.

She's not herself. / She's not what she's always like.

She's really shining today.

I fell in love with her again.

These days, dating is getting to be boring. / These days, dating has become monotonous.

Every time we date, we argue.

Whatever we do, it's boring. ⇨ boring=no fun

2人の関係も、もう終わりかな。

描写表現　喧嘩　CD①②22

相手の発言に腹を立てる

人の行為にムカッとくる。

喧嘩をする。

人に喧嘩をしかける。

相手を責める。

人を激しくののしる。

相手にイヤミを言われる。

殴り合いをする。

別れる決意をする。

彼に別れを告げる。

One Point Lesson　食欲について

「食欲」について少し整理してみましょう。the desire for food or drink を表す「食欲」は英語で appetite。「今日は食欲がない」は I have no appetite today. とか、I don't want to eat anything today. とします。また習慣的に「いつも食欲がない」は I have a poor appetite. 反対に「私は食欲旺盛だ」は I have a good appetite. あるいは I have a hearty appetite.、「食欲がなくなった」は I've lost my appetite. です。
　ちなみに、「モリモリ食べる」は I eat with a good appetite.、I eat with a hearty appetite.、「食が進む」は I have a good appetite.、「食欲が出てきた」は My appetite increased. です。

I think it's over for us. / I think we're done with each other.

Descriptive expressions — Argue

I get upset at something the other person says. / I get angry over something somebody said.
⇨ get upset at=get mad at; get angry over ⇨ says → said

I get disgusted at someone's actions. / I get revolted at his behavior. ⇨ someone's → the other person's; his; her

I argue. / I fight.

I pick a fight with someone. ⇨ someone → the other person; him; her

I accuse the other person. ⇨ the other person → him; her

I swear severely at someone. / I violently curse the other person. ⇨ someone → the other person; him; her

I have someone say something sarcastic about me. ⇨ someone → the other person; him; her

I have a fight. / I have a fistfight.

I decide to split up. / I decide to call it quits.

I tell him I'm going to break up with him.

One Point Lesson　手元に

　I don't have any cash with me now.（今、手持ちの現金がない）といった具合に「手元に」「手持ちの」を表す英語は with。ここでの with は、I know a girl with red hair.（私は赤毛の女の子を知っている）のように、所有、具有、携帯、特質などを表して「～を持っている、身に着けて、～した状態で」などの意を表す前置詞です。また with 以外では、I have no money on me.（手持ちのお金はない）といった具合に、with 同様に所有、着用などを表して「～を持って、～を所持して」の意で使われる前置詞 on を使うこともできるのです。

健康

描写表現　病院　　　　　　　　　　　　　　　　　CD① ② 23

病院を探す。

インターネットで良い病院を探す。

病院に電話する。

診察時間を聞く。

予約する。

病院へ行く。

診察室に入る。

医師に胃の調子が悪いことを告げる。

医師の質問に答える。

描写表現　検査

健康診断を受ける。

検査を受ける。

身体検査を受ける。

レントゲン検査を受ける。

体重を測る。

身長を測る。

血圧を測る。

視力検査を受ける。

Health

Descriptive expressions **Hospital**

I look for a hospital.

I search for a good hospital on the Internet. / I look for a good hospital on the Net.
⇨ on the Internet =on the net; on line

I call the hospital. ⇨ call=telephone

I ask about office hours. ⇨ office hours=hours for diagnosis

I make an appointment.

I go to the hospital.

I go into the examination room.

I tell the doctor my stomach is upset. / I tell the doctor I have stomach trouble.

I answer the doctor's questions.

Descriptive expressions **Examination**

I get a check-up. / I have a physical exam.

I am examined.

I have a physical examination.

I have an x-ray taken. / I get an x-ray.

I get weighed. / I weigh myself.

I have my height measured. / I have my height checked.

I have my blood pressure measured. / I measure blood pressure.

I have my vision checked. ⇨ vision=eyesight

朝・午前

昼

午後

夕方

夜

211

血液検査を受ける。

聴覚の検査を受ける。

人間ドッグに入る。

腕に注射される。

インフルエンザワクチンを打ってもらう。

風邪気味なので市販の薬を飲んで寝る。

つぶやき表現　体調　　CD①②24

体の調子が悪い。

疲れやすい。

疲れがとれない。

体がだるい。

筋肉痛だ。

腰が痛い。

最近は運動不足だ。

デスクワークなので、運動不足になりがちだ。

描写表現　眠り

良く眠れない。

すぐに寝てしまう。

いつも眠くて仕方がない。

特に授業中は眠くなる。

I get blood tests.

I have my hearing checked.

I get my comprehensive physical examination.

I get a shot in the arm. ⇨ get a shot=get an injection

I get a flu shot.

As I have a slight cold, I take some over-the-counter medicine and go to bed. ⇨ go to bed=sleep

Mumblings — Physical condition

I don't feel good.

I get tired easily. ⇨ tired=fatigued

I can't get over feeling tired. / I can't recover from fatigue.

I feel sluggish. ⇨ sluggish=lazy

My muscles hurt. ⇨ hurt=ache

My back hurts. / I have a backache.

Lately, I don't get enough exercise. / Lately, I don't exercise enough.

I do desk work, so I tend not to exercise enough.

Descriptive expressions — Sleep

I don't sleep well. ⇨ don't → can't

I fall asleep quickly. ⇨ quickly=fast

I'm always sleepy; it can't be helped.

Especially, I get sleepy in class. ⇨ in class=during lessons

描写表現　気分

気分が悪い。

吐き気がする。

毎日、いらいらする。

最近は怒りっぽい。

描写表現　胃

CD①②25

胃が痛む。

胃に鋭い痛みがある。

空腹時に胃が痛む。

胃がもたれる。

胸焼けする。

描写表現　腰

腰が痛い。

立ち上がるとき腰に激痛が走る。

描写表現　目

目がすぐに疲れる。

目が充血した。

目がかすむ。

遠くのものが見えない。

近くのものがぼやけて見える。

細かい文字が読みにくくなった。

Descriptive expressions — Feeling

I feel sick. / I don't feel good.

I feel nauseous. / I feel sick to my stomach.

I'm jittery every day. ⇨ jittery=annoyed

I get upset these days. ⇨ upset=angry

Descriptive expressions — Stomach

My stomach hurts.

I have a sharp pain in my stomach.

My stomach hurts when it's empty. ⇨ it's empty=I'm hungry

I've got a heavy stomach. / My stomach feels heavy.

I've got heartburn. ⇨ heartburn=indigestion

Descriptive expressions — Back

I have a pain in my back. / I have a backache.

When I stand up I have a shooting pain in my lower back. ⇨ I have=I get ⇨ a shooting pain=a severe pain

Descriptive expressions — Eye

My eyes are easily tired. ⇨ tired=strained

My eyes are bloodshot.

My vision is foggy. / My eyes are blurred.
⇨ foggy=fuzzy ⇨ blurred=cloudy

I can't see things far away. ⇨ far away=at a distance

Close things look fuzzy. ⇨ fuzzy=dim

It's gotten hard to read small print. ⇨ hard=difficult

左目に異物が入った。

右目にものもらいができきた。

描写表現　耳　　　　　　　　　　　　　　　　　　　CD①②26

耳が聞こえない。

高音が聞きにくい。

耳が遠い。

耳鳴りがする。

描写表現　頭

頭が重い。

頭がクラクラする。

頭が痛い。

描写表現　熱

熱がある。

微熱が続いている。

急に熱が出た。

熱を測る。

今、38度の熱がある。

熱が下がらない。

熱が上がったり下がったりする。

顔がほてっている。

熱で体がほてっている。

I've got something in my left eye. ⇨ I've got=I have

I've got a sty in my right eye.

Descriptive expressions **Ear**

I can't hear.

High sounds are hard to hear. ⇨ High sounds= High frequency sounds

I'm hard of hearing.

I have a ringing in my ears. / My ears are ringing.

Descriptive expressions **Head**

My head feels heavy.

My head's spinning. / My head is swimming. / I'm dizzy.

My head hurts. / I have a headache.

Descriptive expressions **Fever**

I've got a fever.

The slight fever is continuing. ⇨ continuing=chronic

I got a fever all of a sudden.

I take my temperature.

I have a fever of 38 degrees.

The fever won't go down. ⇨ go down=break

My fever goes up and down. / It's an undulating fever.

My face feels hot.

I'm burning up with fever.

217

描写表現　喉

喉が痛い。

喉が痛くて、しゃべれない。

物を食べると喉が痛む。

魚の骨が喉に引っかかった。

扁桃腺が腫れている。

描写表現　咳

咳が出る。

咳がひどい。

咳が抜けない。

夜、咳が出て眠れない。

描写表現　風邪

鼻水が出る。

風邪を引いている。

風邪気味だ。

鼻かぜを引いている。

彼女から風邪をうつされた。

風邪で3日間、寝ている。

描写表現　歯

歯が痛い。

酸っぱいものを食べると歯が浮く。

虫歯がある。

Descriptive expressions — Throat

My throat hurts. / I have a sore throat.

My throat's sore and I can't talk.

When I eat, my throat hurts.

A fish bone stuck in my throat.

My tonsils are swollen.

Descriptive expressions — Cough

I cough.

I have a bad cough.

The cough won't go away. / The cough is persistent.

At night I cough and can't sleep. ⇨ can't sleep= can't go to sleep

Descriptive expressions — Cold

My nose runs. / I have a runny nose.

I caught a cold. / I have a cold. ⇨ a cold=cold

I have a slight cold. / I have a bit of cold.

I have a head cold. / I have a cold in the head.

I got my cold from her. / She gave me her cold.

I've been in bed with a cold for three days.

Descriptive expressions — Tooth

I have a toothache. ⇨ I have=I've got

Whenever I eat something sour, it sets my teeth on edge. ⇨ sets my teeth on edge=sets my teeth tingle

I have a cavity. ⇨ a cavity=dental caries

奥歯が 1 本虫歯になっている。

歯が 1 本抜けそうになっている。

虫歯を治療してもらう。

虫歯を抜いてもらう。

口臭がある。

描写表現　便秘

便秘をしている。

1 週間ほど便通がない。

描写表現　体重

体重が落ちた。

ここ 1 か月で体重が 10 キロも落ちた。

急に太りだした。

半年の間に 15 キロも太った。

描写表現　血圧

CD①②29

血圧が高い。

血圧が低い。

血糖値は正常だ。

描写表現　その他の表現

食欲がない。

I've got a cavity on one of my molars.

It looks like one of my teeth is gonna come out.
⇨ come out=fall out

I have my cavity filled.

I have my decayed tooth pulled.

I have bad breath. ⇨ bad breath=halitosis

Descriptive expressions — Constipation

I'm constipated.

I haven't had a stool in about a week. / I haven't defecated for nearly one week. ⇨ I haven't had= I haven't passed

Descriptive expressions — Weight

I've lost weight.

I've lost ten kilos already in the past month.
⇨ past month=last month

I've gained weight suddenly.

I've gained 15 kilos in half a year.
⇨ in half a year=in a half year

Descriptive expressions — Blood pressure

My blood pressure's high. / I have high blood pressure. ⇨ high blood pressure=hypertension

My blood pressure's low.

My blood sugar's normal.

Descriptive expressions — Other expressions

I don't have any appetite. / I have no appetite.

最近、下痢気味だ。

体脂肪率は 10％前後だ。

生理痛がひどい。

足の関節がときどき痛む。

描写表現　肌　　　　　　　　　　　　　CD①②30

肌が荒れている。

化粧品で肌がかぶれた。

体中に湿疹ができた。

顔にニキビができた。

頬のホクロが気になる。

皮膚炎だ。

描写表現　その他の表現

体を引き締める。

体を鍛えるためにジムに通う。

体重を落とす。

ダイエットを始める。

体重を 10 キロ落としたために、服を買い替える。

ダイエットして、ベルトの穴 3 つ分細くなる。

ダイエットの後、リバウンドする。

太ったので体のラインが崩れる。

Lately, I'm prone to diarrhea. / I tend to get diarrhea recently.

My body fat ratio is about 10 percent.

The menstrual pain is tough. / The menstrual cramps are severe.

The joints in my feet hurt sometimes. / My legs hurt sometimes.

Descriptive expressions Skin

My skin's rough.

I have a rash due to cosmetics. ⇨ due to=caused by

I have a rash all over. ⇨ all over=all over my body

I've got a pimple on my face. / I have acne.

I'm concerned about the mole on my cheek.

I get inflammation of the skin. / It's dermatitis.

Descriptive expressions Other expressions

I tone up my body.

I go to the gym to build my body. ⇨ build=train

I lose weight.

I start a diet. ⇨ start=begin

I buy new clothes because I lost 10 kilos.

I diet and tighten up my belt three holes.

I rebound after dieting. ⇨ after dieting=after a diet

I lose body lines because of being fat.
⇨ body lines=definition

体重が増えたため、今までの服が着られない。

One Point Lesson 　歯について

「一本の歯」は tooth ですが、「二本以上の歯」になると teeth。「前歯」は a front tooth、「奥歯」は a back tooth、「糸切歯」は a canine、a dog-tooth、an eye tooth、「乳歯」は a deciduous tooth、a milk tooth、a baby tooth、a temporary tooth、「永久歯」は a permanent tooth、「親知らず」は a wisdom tooth、「臼歯」は a molar tooth、「小臼歯」は a premolar tooth、「門歯」は an incisor、an incisor tooth、「虫歯」は a decayed tooth、a bad tooth、「入れ歯」は a false tooth、an artificial tooth、「歯並び」は teeth alignment。

One Point Lesson 　「痛み」の種類

「痛み」を表す英語はたくさんあります。中でも最も一般的なのが pain。この語は病気、怪我などによる弱い痛みから強い痛み、肉体的、精神的を問わずあらゆる痛みに用いられます。たとえば、「軽い痛み」slight pain、「激しい痛み」は sharp pain、acute pain、bad pain、great pain、intense pain、severe pain、violent pain。「鈍い痛み」dull pain、「ズキズキする痛み」throbbing pain、「キリキリする痛み」piercing pain、「刺すような痛み」stabbing pain、「頑固な痛み」persistent pain、steady pain、「慢性的な痛み」chronic pain、constant pain。

また、「痛みを感じる」は feel pain、experience pain、「痛みを我慢する」は bear pain、stand pain、endure pain、「痛みを和らげる」は ease pain、kill pain、relieve pain、soothe pain、allay pain。ちなみに、他の痛みを表す言葉 ache は部分的な痛みを言い、I have a headache.（頭痛がする）のように、しばしば痛む場所を示す語と合成語を作ります。pang は突然の激痛、twinge は刺すような痛み、smart はズキズキする痛み、sorrow、grief は心の痛みを表現します。

I gained weight, so now I can't wear what I used to. ⇨ what I used to=what I wore up until now

One Point Lesson 　風邪をひく

　この表現は catch cold、または catch a cold。両者の違いは、単に風邪を引いた場合は cold でオーケーですが、I caught a bad cold.（ひどい風邪をひいちゃった）のように、cold に形容詞などの修飾語が伴う場合には、通例、a を付けます。そのため、「軽い風邪をひいた」は I caught a slight cold.、「鼻かぜをひいた」は I caught a cold in the head.、I caught a head cold. あるいは I caught a cold in the nose.、「咳風邪をひいた」は I caught a cold in the chest. となります。

One Point Lesson 　お金にまつわる諺

　Money はどの国でも、またどの時代においてもなくては生きていけない極めて重要なものだけに、この語にまつわる英語の諺は数多くあります。なかでも頻繁に使われるのが Money talks.（金がもの言う）、Money answers all things.（金は全てのことに応ずる→金がもの言う）、Money will do anything.（金はどんなことでもするだろう→金さえあれば飛ぶ鳥も落ちる）、Jack would be a gentleman if he had money.（金があればジャックも紳士になれる→金があれば馬鹿も旦那）、Money will make the pot boil.（金は鍋を煮えたぎらせる→地獄の沙汰も金次第）、Money makes all right that is wrong.（金は間違っているものを正しいことにする→地獄の沙汰も金次第）、Money is the best lawyer.（金は最高の弁護士である→地獄の沙汰も金次第）、Money and good manners make the gentleman.（金と作法は紳士を作る→衣食足りて礼節を知る）、Money is a great traveler in the world.（金は世界の偉大な旅行者である→金は天下の回りもの）、Money begets money.（金が金を産む→金が金を儲ける）。また、金銭が絡んだスキャンダルなどに言及する際には Money is the root of all evils.（金は諸悪の根源）。

Chapter 4 夕方

描写表現 退社する　　　　　　　　　　　　　　　　　　　CD①31

5時に退社する。

毎日5時になると、すぐに退社する。

退社は8時過ぎだ。

いつも仕事が忙しくて、毎日、退社は10時前後だ。

省エネのため、従業員全員が6時までには退社する

つぶやき表現 退社する

たまには早く退社したい。

早く退社して家族のもとへ帰りたい。

毎日、残業なんて嫌になる。

経理課の連中は早く帰れて羨ましい。

Evening

Descriptive expressions — Leaving the office / Leaving work

I quit work at 5. / I go home at five.
⇨ quit work=quit working　⇨ at 5=at 5 o'clock

Every day at five o'clock I leave the company.
⇨ company=office

I leave the company after 8 o'clock.

I'm always busy, so I leave the company around 10 o'clock every day.

To save energy, all employees leave the office by 6 o'clock. / To conserve energy, all of the workers leave the company by 6 o'clock. ⇨ save=conserve

Mumblings — Leaving the office / Leaving work

I wanna quit early sometimes. / I'd like to leave the office early once in a while.
⇨ once in a while=every now and then ; sometimes

I wanna leave work early and get back to my family. / I want to leave work soon and return to the family.

I hate working overtime every day. / Working overtime every day sucks.

I envy the accounting section people who leave early. / I'm jealous of the accounting staff who leave early. ⇨ section=department　⇨ leave=go home

料理

描写表現 献立

今夜の献立を考える。

今夜は何を食べたいか夫に聞く。

今日の昼は簡単な料理ですませる。

手のかかる料理は作らない。

ときどき料理で手抜きをする。

つぶやき表現 料理について

私は料理が得意だ。

私の得意料理はステーキだ。

私は現在、料理の勉強をしている。

私は料理を作るのが嫌い。

私には得意料理はない。

料理するなんて面倒くさいな。

今夜は外食しよう。

描写表現 料理する

台所に行く。

まな板を取り出す。

包丁を取り出す。

Cooking / Cuisine

Descriptive expressions | **Menu**

I plan tonight's menu.

I ask my husband what he wants to eat tonight.

I make a simple lunch today. / I do something simple for lunch today.
⇨ do something simple=make something simple

I won't make something that takes a lot of work. ⇨ a lot of work → a lot of time

Sometimes, I cut corners in cooking.
⇨ Sometimes=Now and then

Mumblings | **About cooking**

I'm good at cooking. / I'm a good cook.

My best dish is steak.

I'm studying cooking now.

I hate to cook. / I really don't like cooking.

I don't have a best dish. / I'm not good at cooking anything special. ⇨ anything special=in particular

It's a lot of trouble to cook. / Cooking is a pain in the neck. ⇨ neck=butt

I'll eat out tonight.

Descriptive expressions | **Cooking**

I go to the kitchen.

I take out the chopping board
⇨ chopping board =chopping block; cutting board

I take out a kitchen knife. ⇨ kitchen knife=butcher knife

描写表現　夕食

夕食の準備に取り掛かる。

冷蔵庫から食材を出す。

夕食を作る。

夕食を食べる。

食後の後片付けをする。

下ごしらえの表現

描写表現　洗う

CD①②34

野菜を洗う。

米をすすぎ洗いする。

ほうれん草の水気を取る。

描写表現　むく

玉ねぎの皮をむく。

ナシの皮をむく。

包丁でジャガイモの皮をむく。

描写表現　取り除く

魚をした処理する。

魚のうろこを取る。

豆のさやを取る。

魚の内臓を取る。

七面鳥の骨を取る。

Descriptive expressions — Dinner / Supper

I prepare for dinner. / I make preparation to fix dinner.

I take the ingredients out of the fridge. ⇨ ingredients → food

I make dinner. ⇨ make=fix; cook

I eat supper.

I clean up after eating. ⇨ after eating=after the meal

Preparation expressions

Descriptive expressions — Wash

I wash the vegetables.

I rinse the rice.

I drain the spinach.

Descriptive expressions — Peel / Pare

I peel the onions.

I pare the Japanese pear.

I peel the potatoes with a kitchen knife.

Descriptive expressions — Getting rid of

I dress the fish.

I scale the fish.

I remove the peas from the pods. / I scale the peas.

I clean the fish.

I bone the turkey.

231

描写表現　切る

かぼちゃを半分に切る。

リンゴを3分の1に切る。

ナシを4分の1に切る。

タケノコを縦に切る。

きゅうりを薄く切る。

大根を薄切りにする。

ニンジンをさいの目に切る。

キャベツをみじん切りにする。

キャベツを千切りにする。

キャベツを刻む。

ニンジンをくさび形に切る。

豚肉をぶつ切りにする。

アジを切り刻む。

描写表現　水を切る

ほうれん草の水を切る。

米のとぎ汁を切る。

スパゲティの水分を切る。

描写表現　その他の表現

鮭を薄切りにする。

マグロを刺身にする。

Descriptive expressions **Cut**

I cut the pumpkin into two halves. / I cut the pumpkin in two. ⇨ into two halves=in half

I cut the apple into thirds.

I cut the pear into quarters.

I cut the bamboo sprout lengthwise.
⇨ bamboo sprout=bamboo shoot

I cut the cucumber into thin slices.

I slice the Japanese radish.

I cut the carrot into cubes. / I dice the carrot.

I cut the cabbage into tiny pieces.

I cut the cabbage into shreds. / I shred the cabbage.

I chop the cabbage.

I cut the carrot into wedges.

I chop the pork.

I chop up the horse mackerel.

Descriptive expressions **Strain**

I strain the water from spinach. ⇨ strain the water from =strain

I strain the water from the rice.

I strain the spaghetti. ⇨ strain=drain

Descriptive expressions **Other expressions**

I cut the salmon into thin slices. / I thinly slice the salmon.

I make tuna sashimi.

ジャガイモをつぶす。

ジャガイモをゆでてつぶす。

大根を下ろす。

チーズを下ろす。

ニンニクを下ろす。

スープをこして取る。

肉汁をこす。

ジャガイモを裏ごしする。

冷凍食品を解凍する。

タケノコのアクを抜く。

クリームを泡立てる。

砂糖をふるいにかける。

サラダを和える。

豆を一晩中水につける。

描写表現　焼く　　　　　　　　　　　CD①②37

ケーキを焼く。

パンをオーブンで焼く。

パンをきつね色に焼く。

トーストをカリカリにする。

魚を焼く。

鶏肉を直火で焼く。

鶏肉をオーブンで焼く。

I **mash the potatoes.** ⇨ the → some

I **boil some potatoes and mash them.**

I **grate a daikon.** ⇨ a daikon= a Japanese radish; a giant white radish

I **grate some cheese.**

I **grate some garlic.**

I **strain the soup.** ⇨ soup=broth

I **strain the gravy.**

I **puree some potatoes.** ⇨ puree=strain

I **defrost the frozen food.**

I **remove the harshness from the bamboo shoots.** ⇨ harshness=scum

I **whip some cream.** ⇨ whip=beat; whisk

I **sift the sugar.**

I **toss a salad.** ⇨ toss=mix

I **soak the beans in water overnight.**

> Descriptive expressions **Bake / Broil / Grill**

I **bake a cake.**

I **bake bread in an oven.**

I **toast some bread.** / I **bake bread to a beautiful brown.**

I **make crispy toast.** / I **crisp toast.**

I **bake some fish.** ⇨ bake=broil

I **broil the chicken.** ⇨ broil=grill

I **roast a chicken in an oven.** ⇨ a chicken → some chicken

235

> 描写表現　**煮る**

野菜を煮る。

シチューをとろ火で煮る。

肉をとろ火で煮る。

肉と野菜を蒸し煮する。

トマトソースを半分になるまで煮詰める。

> 描写表現　**揚げる**

エビに衣を付ける。

豚肉にパン粉をまぶす。

鶏肉に小麦粉をまぶす。

ゴーヤを揚げる。

ポテトをからっと揚げる。

> 描写表現　**炒める**　　　　　　　　　CD①②38

フライパンでバターを溶かす。

玉ねぎをバターで少し茶色になるまで炒める。

野菜を油で炒める。

玉ねぎを3分炒める。

肉と野菜を強火でさっと炒める。

ジャガイモを揚げる。

カキを揚げる。

冷めた料理を温め直す。

Descriptive expressions **Boil**

I boil the vegetables.

I simmer the stew.

I stew meat.

I braise some meat and veggies. ⇨veggies=vegetables

I boil down the tomato-sauce to half the volume.
⇨boil down=reduce

Descriptive expressions **Deep fry**

I dip a shrimp into some batter.

I bread the pork chops.

I dust the chicken with flour. / I dredge the chicken in flour.

I deep-fry sour melons. ⇨sour melon=bitter melon

I deep-fry potatoes until they are crisp.

Descriptive expressions **Stir fry / Pan fry**

I melt some butter in the pan.

I brown some onions with the butter lightly. / I lightly caramelize some onions with the butter.

I saute vegetables in oil.

I pan-fry the onions for three minutes.

I stir-fry the meat and vegetables. ⇨ vegetables=veggies

I french-fry potatoes.

I deep-fry oysters.

I warm up the cold food. ⇨warm up=warm over ; rewarm

237

つぶやき表現　SOS 表現

魚を焦がしてしまった。

この肉は焼けすぎだ。

牛肉を煮過ぎた。

この肉は生焼きだ。

このサバは生煮えだ。

スープを吹きこぼしちゃった。

描写表現　ゆでる

ブロッコリをゆでる。

アスパラガスをしんなりするまでゆでる。

ほうれん草をゆがく。

ジャガイモを蒸す。

サツマイモをふかす。

描写表現　卵料理

卵をゆでる。

卵を固くゆでる。

卵を半熟にする。

卵を短時間ゆでる。

卵を割る。

卵をかき混ぜる。

タマゴ焼きを作る。

目玉焼きを作る。

両面焼きを作る。

タマゴご飯を作る。

(Mumblings) SOS expressions

I burnt the fish.

This meat is overcooked.

I overcooked the beef. ⇨ overcooked=boiled too long; boiled too much

This meat is undercooked. ⇨ undercooked=raw

This mackerel is undercooked.

The soup boiled over.

Descriptive expressions Boil

I boil broccoli.

I boil asparagus until tender.

I blanch spinach. ⇨ blanch=parboil

I steam potatoes.

I steam sweet-potatoes.

Descriptive expressions Egg dishes

I boil eggs. ⇨ eggs → an egg

I hard boil an egg.

I soft boil eggs.

I poach eggs.

I break an egg. / I crack an egg open.

I beat eggs. / I whisk eggs.

I fry eggs. / I make a fried egg.

I make eggs sunny-side up.

I fry an egg overeasy.

I make rice topped with raw egg and soy sauce.

描写表現　まぜる　　　　　　　　　　CD②39

スープをかき混ぜる。

コーヒーに砂糖を入れてかき混ぜる。

野菜サラダを軽くかき混ぜる。

卵白をよくかき回して泡立てる。

ボールの中で材料をかき混ぜる。

小麦粉に砂糖と塩を少し加える。

小麦粉、牛乳、卵を混ぜてホットケーキを作る。

描写表現　味付け

料理にコショウをふりかける。

スープにクレソンをふりかける。

牛肉にコショウをふりかける。

豚肉に小麦粉をふりかける。

牛肉に塩コショウする。

ヒレ肉に赤ワインをかける。

マカロニをトマトソースで味付けする。

料理にレモンを飾り付ける。

料理に野菜を盛り付ける。

チキン出汁3杯分を加える。

テーブルスプーン2杯分のハチミツを加える。

カレーにヨーグルト1カップ半を加える。

Descriptive expressions **Mix**

I stir the soup.

I stir sugar into my coffee.

I toss a green salad.

I beat the egg whites well.

I mix ingredients in a bowl.

I mix some sugar and salt into the flour.

I mix flour, milk, and eggs and make pancakes. / I blend flour, milk, and eggs to make the pancake. ⇨ pancakes=hotcakes; flapjacks

Descriptive expressions **Season**

I sprinkle pepper on a dish.

I sprinkle the soup with watercress.

I dust pepper on beef.

I dust pork with flour.

I salt and pepper beef. / I season beef with salt and pepper.

I pour red wine over the fillets.

I season macaroni with tomato sauce.

I garnish the dish with lemon.

I dish up the vegetables.

I add three cups of chicken stock.

I add two tablespoons of honey.

I add one and a half cups of yogurt to the curry.

味

つぶやき表現 おいしい　　　　　　　　　　　　CD②40

これはおいしい。

これは濃厚な味だ。

これは甘い。

これはちょうどいい味だ。

これはまあまあだな。

つぶやき表現 まずい

これはまずいな。

これはしょっぱい。

これは塩味が効きすぎている。

これは辛すぎる。

これは辛すぎて、舌がヒリヒリする。

これは苦い。

これは少し酸っぱい。

これは全然味がしない。

これは味が薄い。

これは味が濃すぎる。

つぶやき表現 コク

この料理はこくがある。

このワインにはこくがある。

つぶやき表現 調理失敗　　　　　　　　　　　　CD②41

これは生ぬるい。

Flavor

Mumblings Delicious

This is delicious. ⇨ delicious=tasty; good; nice; great

This is rich. / This tastes rich.

This is sweet.

This tastes perfect. ⇨ perfect=just right

This is so so. ⇨ so so=mediocre

Mumblings Not good

This does not taste good. / This tastes bad. / This is terrible. / This sucks.

This is salty.

This is too salty.

This is too spicy. ⇨ spicy=hot

This is too spicy. It makes my tongue tingle. ⇨ tingle=burn

This is bitter.

This is a bit sour. ⇨ sour=acidic; acid

This is tasteless.

This tastes bland.

This tastes too rich.

Mumblings Body

This food has body.

This wine is full-bodied.

Mumblings Cooking failures

This is lukewarm. / This is not hot enough. ⇨ lukewarm=tepid

243

これは熱すぎる。

これは冷えていない。

これは脂っこい。

焦げた臭いがする。

これ焦がしちゃった。

これは生焼けだ。

これはよく焼けていない。

これはかび臭い。

このビールは気が抜けている。

これは腐っている。

これはぬるぬるしている。

これは硬くて噛みきれない。

描写表現　調理器具　CD② 42

オーブンを使う。

オーブンのスイッチを入れる。

料理するために電子レンジを使う。

電子レンジのコードを入れる。

電子レンジを 10 分に設定する。

オーブンを予熱する。

描写表現　火

火をおこす。

火を消す。

This is too hot.

This isn't cold enough.

This is greasy. ⇨greasy=oily

This smells burnt.

I burnt this.

This is soggy.

This isn't baked well. ⇨baked=roasted; grilled

This is musty.

This beer is flat.

This is rotten. ⇨rotten=spoiled

This is slimy.

This is too tough to chew.

Descriptive expressions ▶ Cooking utensils / Cooking tools

I use an oven.

I turn on the oven. / I turn the oven on. / I push the oven's start switch.

I use a microwave for cooking. / I cook with a microwave oven.

I plug in the microwave.

I set the microwave oven for ten minutes.

I preheat the oven.

Descriptive expressions ▶ Fire

I make a fire.

I put out a fire.

強火にする。

火力を増す。

電子レンジを強火にする。

弱火にする。

火を止める。

やかんを火にかける。

材料を深鍋に入れて弱火にかける。

弱火でぐつぐつ煮る。

野菜を強火で炒める。

描写表現　炊く

電気ガマでご飯を炊く。

3人分のご飯を炊く。

2人分の料理を作る。

描写表現　温める

日本酒を温める。

冷えたスープを温める。

電子レンジで冷めたご飯を温める。

描写表現　冷やす

ビールを冷やす。

料理を冷ます。

描写表現　その他の表現

フライパンの中で玉子をひっくり返す。

I turn up the heat. / I set the gas high.

I increase the flame to high.

I set the microwave on high heat.

I turn down the heat.

I turn off the heat.

I put a kettle on the fire.

I put the ingredients in a saucepan over low heat. ⇨over=on

I simmer over a low fire. ⇨fire=flame

I fry the vegetables over a high flame.

Descriptive expressions Cook

I cook rice in an electric cooker.

I make rice for three people.

I cook for two people. ⇨for two people=for two

Descriptive expressions Warm up

I warm up the sake. ⇨warm up=heat

I warm up cold soup.

I warm up cold rice in a microwave.

Descriptive expressions Chill

I chill some beer.

I cool the food.

Descriptive expressions Other expressions

I turn over the eggs in the frying pan.
⇨turn over=turn ⇨frying pan=skillet

牛乳の乳脂をすくい取る。

オーブントースターでグラタンに焦げ目をつける。

カレーを一晩寝かせる。

チーズを溶かす。

描写表現　給仕　　　　　　　　　　　　　　　CD①②44

料理を皿に載せる。

ご飯をよそう。

ご飯を茶碗に入れる。

料理を出す。

料理を盆に載せる。

料理をテーブルに並べる。

描写表現　その他の表現

ご飯をおかわりする。

出された料理を完食する。

料理を残す。

残った料理にサランラップをかける。

描写表現　冷蔵庫　　　　　　　　　　　　　　CD①②45

冷蔵庫のドアを開ける。

冷蔵庫から食材を取り出す。

冷蔵庫で缶コーヒーを冷やす。

冷凍庫に冷凍食品を入れる。

I skim the cream from milk.

I sear gratin with the oven toaster. ⇨ oven toaster= toaster oven

I let curry stand overnight.

I melt the cheese.

Descriptive expressions Table service

I put dishes on the table. / I set the table. ⇨ dishes =plates

I fill the rice bowls. / I serve rice.

I put rice in the bowls.

I serve the food.

I put the food on a tray.

I arrange the food on a table. / I line up the dishes on a table.

Descriptive expressions Other expressions

I have a second serving of rice. / I have seconds of rice.

I eat all of the food served. / I eat everything they serve. ⇨ food=dishes ⇨ serve=put out

I leave food. / I leave food on my plate.

I cover the leftovers with Saran wrap. / I put Saran wrap over the leftover food.

Descriptive expressions Fridge / Refrigerator

I open the refrigerator door.

I take the ingredients out of the fridge.

I chill canned coffee in the fridge.

I put frozen food in the freezer.

249

冷蔵庫で残った料理を保存する。

牛肉を冷凍保存する。

冷蔵庫で氷を作る。

冷蔵庫のドアを閉める。

冷蔵庫のドアの開閉を速やかに行なう。

つぶやき表現　**冷蔵庫**

冷蔵庫の中は物で一杯だな。

たしか、冷蔵庫の中にジャムが入っていたはずだが。

あれ、こんな物が入っていた。

これ、いつ買ったんだろう。

賞味期限が切れている。

このソーセージ、2年前に買っているな。

冷蔵庫の中が匂う。

新しい防臭剤を入れないといけない。

そろそろ防臭剤を交換する時期だな。

One Point Lesson　「長所」を英語で言うと

　「長所」に対応する最も一般的な英語は strong point と good point で、他より優れている点のこと。同様の意で advantage があります。この語は他よりも「有利な点、有利な立場、強味」を表します。He is a man of merit.（彼は優秀な人物だ）のように、merit は尊敬、賞賛に値する「優秀さ、長所」、すなわち a good quality that makes something deserve praise or admiration のこと。また She has the virtue of knowing her weakness.（彼女には自分の弱点を知っているという長所がある）といった具合に、virtue は「美徳」の他に、物事、性格などの「長所、美点」を表して使われる語です。

I keep leftover food in the refrigerator. ⇨ keep=store

I freeze beef. / I keep beef in the freezer.

I make ice in the fridge.

I shut the refrigerator door. ⇨ shut=close

I quickly open and close the refrigerator door.

(Mumblings) Fridge / Refrigerator

The fridge is full of stuff. / The refrigerator is full.

I'm sure there was some jam in the fridge. / There must be some jam in the refrigerator.

Hey, this was in there.

I wonder when I bought this.

The "Best before" date is past. / It's past the "Eat before" date.

I bought these sausages two years ago.

The fridge smells. / The inside of the refrigerator has a bad odor.

I'll have to put in some new odor eaters. ⇨ odor eaters=deodorizer

It's about time to change the odor eater. ⇨ change=replace

One Point Lesson turn on

この表現は She turned on the radio.（彼女はラジオをつけた）、She turned on the light.（彼女は明かりをつけた）、She turned on the water.（彼女は水を出した）のように、明かり、火、ラジオ、テレビ、ガス、水など一般的に栓やスイッチを回してつけたり、物資を供給するものについて「つける、出す、始める」などの意を表して使われます。

反対に「消す、とめる」とする場合は、She turned off the engine.（彼女はエンジンを切った）のように turn off となります。

描写表現　虫について　　　　　　　　　　　　CD ① ② 46

部屋にハエが入ってくる。

部屋の中でハエが飛び回っている。

ハエが壁に止っている。

ハエが食べ物に止る。

机の下にゴキブリがいる。

窓を開けた瞬間にカが入ってきた。

カに腕を刺される。

防虫スプレーを探す。

カの駆除剤をかける。

カに刺されたところに薬をぬる。

かゆみ止めの薬をぬる。

ハエを叩く。

ゴキブリを追いかける。

ゴキブリを部屋の片隅に追い詰める。

ゴキブリに手元にあった本を投げつける。

描写表現　クリーニング　　　　　　　　　　　CD ① ② 47

夏物の衣服をクリーニングに出す。

クリーニング店で汚れた個所を説明する。

汚れの原因を説明する。

油汚れであることを説明する。

シミ取りをお願いする。

スーツをクリーニング店から取ってくる。

Descriptive expressions **About bugs**

A fly gets into the house. ⇨ A fly gets → Some flies get

Flies are flying around in the room.

Flies are on the walls.

Flies land on the food.

There's a cockroach under the desk. ⇨ cockroach=roach

When I opened a window, a mosquito came in.

A mosquito bites my arm.

I look for some insect spray. ⇨ insect spray=insect repellent

I spray mosquito repellent.

I apply medicine on the mosquito bite. ⇨ apply=spread

I put on anti-itch medicine. / I apply medicine to relieve the itching.

I swat flies.

I chase roaches. / I go after roaches.

I cram the cockroaches into a corner of the room.

I throw a nearby book at the roach.

Descriptive expressions **Dry cleaning / Cleaning**

I take the summer clothes to the cleaner's.

I explain the dirty places to the cleaner's. ⇨ dirty=soiled

I explain the cause of the dirty places. ⇨ dirty=soiled

I explain the dirty oil. ⇨ dirty oil=grease spots

I ask them to remove the stains.

I pick up suits from the cleaner's. ⇨ pick up=get

253

スーツがきれいになっていることを確認する。

描写表現 **SOS 表現**

シミが取れていない。

シャツの襟の汚れが取れていない。

スカートの油汚れが全く取れていない。

白いシャツの汚れが以前より広がっている。

シャツの汚れが前よりひどくなっているように思える。

クリーニング店に苦情を言いに行く。

クリーニング店で汚れが落ちていないことを説明する。

シャツのボタンが1つ無くなっていることを伝える。

描写表現 **買い物** CD①②48

買い物に行く。

近くのスーパーへ行く。

駅前の商店街へ行く。

商品の豊富な大型店へ行く。

品質の良いものを置いている店へ行く。

I confirm the suits are clean.

> Descriptive expressions SOS expressions

Stains haven't been removed. / There are still stains.

The stain on the collar of the shirt is still there.
⇨ stain on the collar=dirt on the neck ⇨ still there=didn't come out

The oil stains haven't been removed from the skirt. ⇨ oil=grease

The dirt on the white shirt has gotten bigger.
⇨ gotten bigger=gotten worse

I think the stains on the shirt are much worse than before.

I go to the cleaner's to complain.

I explain to the cleaner's that the dirt hasn't been removed.

I tell them that a button is missing from the shirt.

> Descriptive expressions Shopping

I go shopping.

I go to a nearby supermarket. ⇨ a → the

I go to the shopping arcade in front of the station.

I go to a big store full of goods. ⇨ goods=products

I go to a shop filled with good quality things.
⇨ shop=store

新鮮な野菜を置いている八百屋へ行く。

安くて良い品物を置いている主婦に人気の店へ行く。

描写表現　店内

店の中を見て回る。

買物かごを持って店内をゆっくり歩く。

ショッピングカートを押す。

鮮魚コーナーへ行く。

雑貨コーナーで立ち止まる。

リンゴを1つ手に取る。

手に取ったリンゴと他のリンゴを比べる。

より新鮮な方のリンゴを買う。

ミカンを1袋買う。

つぶやき表現　店内　　　　　　　　　　CD①②49

この店は品数が豊富だ。

この店には何でもあるじゃないか。

こんなものまで置いてある。

みな高いものばかりだ。

今日は何が安いかな？

この牛乳、3割引だ。

I go to a grocery store that has fresh veggies.
⇨veggies=vegetables

I go to a shop with cheap, good quality goods popular with house wives.

>Descriptive expressions> Inside the shop

I walk around the store, looking around.

I walk through the shop carrying a shopping basket.

I push a shopping cart.

I go to the fresh fish corner.

I stop at the sundries corner. ⇨sundries corner= convenience goods section

I pick up an apple.

I compare the apple I picked up to another one.
⇨to=with ⇨another one=another apple

I buy the fresher apple.

I buy a bag of tangerines. ⇨tangerines=mandarin oranges

>Mumblings> Inside the shop

This shop has an abundance of items. / This store has a lot of goods. ⇨shop=store

This shop has everything, doesn't it?

They even have this. / They even have these kinds of things.

Everything's expensive.

I wonder what's cheap today.

This milk is 30% off. / This milk is marked down 30 percent.

257

たまご1パックお1人様80円だって。

2パック目からは100円か。

この刺身は新鮮かな？

パックの底に赤い汁が出ているから新鮮じゃないな。

> つぶやき表現　**古い**

このキャベツ、少し古い感じがする。

これは収穫してからだいぶ時間が経過しているな。

あと数日したら腐るかも。

ヘタの部分が茶色っぽくなっている。

> つぶやき表現　**賞味期限**

この弁当の賞味期限は今日の夕方だ。

新鮮なのはないかな。

こちらの方が新鮮だな。

こっちの弁当の賞味期限は明日の朝だ。

とにかく新鮮な方を選ばないとね。

賞味期限が近いものは買わないよ。

どの店でも古いものを上に、新しいものを下に置くんだよね。

だまされないぞ。

Eggs are 80 yen per pack for one person.

They're 100 yen from the second pack.

Is this sashimi fresh? ⇨ sashimi=sliced raw fish

The bottom of the pack has red liquid coming out, so it's not fresh. ⇨ liquid=juice

Mumblings Old

This cabbage seems a little old. ⇨ seems=feels

This was picked a long time ago. ⇨ picked=harvested

It'll probably rot in a few days.

The bottom part has turned brown.

Mumblings The best by date

The eat by date of this Bento is tonight.
⇨ The eat by date = The best by date ⇨ tonight=this evening

Don't they have anything fresh?

This one is fresh. / This one is more fresh.

The eat by date of this Bento is tomorrow morning. ⇨ The eat by date=The best by date

Anyway, I'll have to buy a fresh one. / At any rate, I'll have to buy fresh ones.

I don't buy anything if the eat by date is close.
⇨ I don't = I won't ⇨ close = soon

All the stores put the old things on top and the new ones on the bottom.

I won't be fooled. ⇨ fooled=tricked

259

> 描写表現　**衣料品売り場**　　　CD①②50

衣料品売り場へ向かう。

ドレスについて店員に尋ねる。

流行のデザインについて聞く。

格子模様のスカートを選ぶ。

試着室を探す。

Mサイズのスカートを試着する。

ウエストが小さいのでMサイズのスカートを元の場所に戻す。

Lサイズのスカートに代える。

> つぶやき表現　**色**

この色は素敵だな。

このドレス、色がきれいだ。

これと同じものでブルーのものが欲しい。

同じ模様で赤いのを探してるんだけど。

これと、あれ、どっちがいいかな？

赤と黒、どっちが私に似合うかな？

> つぶやき表現　**デザイン**　　　CD①②51

このコートかっこいいな。

この服、おしゃれだな。

Descriptive expressions **Clothing department**

I head for the clothing department.
⇨ clothing department=apparel counter

I ask a clerk about a dress.

I ask about popular designs.
⇨ popular designs=designs in fashion

I choose a lattice pattern skirt. / I select a plaid skirt.

I look for a dressing room.

I try on a medium sized skirt.

The waist is small, so I return the M size skirt to its place.

I change to an L size skirt.

Mumblings **Color**

This is a pretty color. / This color is pretty.

The color of this dress is beautiful. / I love the color of this dress.

I want one just like this in blue. / I want a blue one just like this.

I'm looking for a red one with the same pattern.

Which is better, this one or that?

Which suits me better, red or black?

Mumblings **Design**

This is a nice coat.

This clothing is fashionable. ⇨ fashionable=dressy

これらの服はデザインがいいね。

これは着心地がすごくいい。

これを着るとスタイルが良く見える。

これ、私に似合うかな？

つぶやき表現　**サイズ**

このサイズは私には少し大きい気がする。

ひとつ下のサイズを試してみよう。

もう少し大きいサイズのものはないかな。

Lサイズはあるのに M サイズはいつも売り切れだよ。

これ、私にピッタリだと思う。

これに決めた。

つぶやき表現　**値段**　　　　　　　　　　　CD①②52

手ごろな値段だ。

この値段なら、私にも買える。

つぶやき表現　**高い**

これ、こんなに高いの？

この小さなバッグが 50 万円だって？

こんなに高いんじゃ、とても手がでない。

誰がこんなに高いものを買うのだろう？

These clothes have nice designs. ⇨nice=good

The fit and feel of this is very good.
⇨is very good=are great

When I wear this, I look very stylish.

Does this look good on me? / I wonder if this suits me. ⇨Does → Would

Mumblings Size

I think this size is a little too big for me.

I'll try on one size smaller.

I wonder if they have a little bigger size.
⇨bigger=larger

They have L sizes, but the M sizes are always sold out.

I think this is just right for me. ⇨right=perfect

I'll buy this. / I'll get this.

Mumblings Price

That's a reasonable price. ⇨reasonable=moderate

At this price, even I can buy this.

Mumblings Expensive

This is so expensive? / This costs that much?

I can't believe this small bag is half a million yen. ⇨bag is=bag costs ⇨half a million yen=500 thousand yen

At this high price, I really can't afford it.
⇨afford it=buy it

I wonder who buys such expensive things.

つぶやき表現 　**安い**

もう少し安いのがいい。

値切ってみようかな。

こういう店では、まけてくれないだろうな。

これは安い。

これ、安すぎるよ。

どうしてこんなに安く売ることができるのだろう？

つぶやき表現 　**どこの製品**　　　　　　　　　　CD①②53

これ、どこの国の製品だろう？

これは輸入品に違いない。

すぐ壊れたりしないだろうね？

品質は保証してくれるのかな？

つぶやき表現 　**SOS 表現**

ウエストが少しきついな。

このシャツ、私には大きすぎる。

腕が長すぎる。

少し胴回りを詰めてもらわないと。

描写表現 　**プレゼント**　　　　　　　　　　CD①②54

友人の誕生日プレゼントを選ぶ。

Mumblings Inexpensive

A little cheaper would be better. ⇨ would be → is

Maybe I'll ask for a discount. / I think I'll bargain for this.

They probably don't give discounts in a shop like this. ⇨ give discounts=cut prices

This is cheap. ⇨ cheap=inexpensive

This is too cheap.

How can they sell this so cheaply?

Mumblings Made in where

I wonder where this was made. / I wonder in which country this was made.

This has got to be an import. / These must be imported goods. ⇨ goods=merchandise

I wonder if it'll break soon. / I hope it won't break soon.

I wonder if they will guarantee the quality.

Mumblings SOS expressions

The waist is a little tight.

This shirt's too big for me.

The sleeves are too long.

Maybe I'll have them take in the girth a little.
⇨ a little=a bit

Descriptive expressions Presents

I pick out a present for my friend's birthday.
⇨ pick out=choose

265

ティファニーの指輪を買う。

プレゼント用に包装してもらう。

子供の服を買う。

描写表現　値切る

バーゲンセールへ行く。

割引されている商品を買う。

シャツが20％引きになっていたので、買う。

鞄を10％割引で買う。

商品の値段を値切る。

15％値切ってみる。

5％まけてもらう。

交渉の結果、10％まけてもらう。

すぐに必要なものではなかったが、安かったので買う。

描写表現　セール

夏物一掃セールが行なわれている。

店じまいのため、全商品が半額になっている。

あの店では2日間、お客様感謝セールが行なわれる。

すべての商品が10％引きになっている。

I buy a ring from Tiffany's. / I buy a Tiffany ring.

I have it **gift-wrapped**.

I buy children's clothes.
⇨ buy children's clothes=buy some children's clothes

Descriptive expressions　Bargain / Discount

I go to bargain sales. / I go to a bargain sale.

I buy some discounted goods. / I buy some marked-down items.

The shirt has been marked down 20 percent, so I buy it.

I buy shoes at a ten percent discount.

I bargain over the price of goods. ⇨ goods=merchandise

I try for a 15 percent discount.

I have them give me 5 percent off.

After negotiating, I get a 10 percent discount.

It was not something I needed, but I bought it because it was cheap.

Descriptive expressions　Sale

They're having a sale on summer goods in one clean sweep.

They're having a going-out-of-business sale, so everything is half price.

That shop is having a customer appreciation sale for two days.

All of the items are 10 percent off.
⇨ 10 percent off=marked down 10 percent

会計

描写表現　支払う

レジに向かう。

レジで代金を払う。

財布から 1 万円札を取り出す。

5,200 円ピッタリ払う。

現金で払う。

レシートを受け取る。

領収書を要求する。

描写表現　お釣り

1 万円からお釣りをもらう。

2,500 円のおつりをもらう。

描写表現　クレジットカード

クレジットカードで払う。

クレジットカードで 1 回払いをする。

クレジットカードで 10 回に分けて払う。

描写表現　ビニールバッグ

プラスチックバッグを 2 枚もらう。

プラスチックバッグをもう 1 枚要求する。

Accounting

Descriptive expressions Pay

I head for the cash register. ⇨ cash register=register

I pay the cost at the register. ⇨ cost=price

I take a ten-thousand yen note out of my wallet. / I take out a ten-thousand yen note from my wallet.

I pay exactly five thousand two hundred yen.
⇨ five thousand two hundred yen=fifty-two hundred yen

I pay cash.

I get a receipt.

I ask for a receipt.

Descriptive expressions Change

I get change from ten thousand yen.

I get two thousand five hundred yen. ⇨ get=receive
⇨ two thousand five hundred yen =twenty-five hundred yen

Descriptive expressions Credit card

I use a credit card. / I pay by credit card. / I pay with my credit card.

I use a one-time payment on my credit card.

I pay in ten installments on my credit card.

Descriptive expressions Plastic bag

I get two plastic bags.

I ask for another plastic bag. ⇨ another=one more

描写表現　詰める

買ったものをバッグに詰める。

買った食料品を持参のバッグに入れる。

描写表現 SOS　その他の表現

これは品質が悪い。

商品が傷ものだ。

買ったバッグに傷があるのを見つける。

買った商品が壊れている。

買った品物を店に返却する。

返金してもらう。

商品を交換してもらう。

おつりの間違いを伝える。

カードの返却を要求する。

描写表現　ネット注文　　　　　　　　　CD①②57

ネットで本を注文する。

アマゾンコムでトム・クルーズ主演の映画の DVD を注文する。

つぶやき表現　ネット注文

ネット通販はいつでも注文できるから便利だ。

真夜中にでも注文できる。

Descriptive expressions — Packing

I pack the things I bought in a bag. ⇨ pack → put

I put groceries I bought in a bag I brought.
⇨ groceries=food

Descriptive expressions — Other expressions

This is poor quality. ⇨ poor=bad

The merchandise is damaged.

I find a tear in the bag I bought.

The items I bought are damaged.

I take the item I bought back to the store. / I return the goods I bought to the store.

I get a refund.

I get a substitute item. / I trade it for a new one.

I tell them they made a mistake with my change.

I ask them to give my card back.

Descriptive expressions — Internet ordering/Online ordering

I order books on the net. ⇨ on the net=on the Net; on the Internet

I order a Tom Cruise film from Amazon.com. / I order a movie Tom Cruise is in from Amazon.com.

Mumblings — Internet ordering/Online ordering

I can order things on the Net anytime, so it's convenient. ⇨ I → You

I can order things even in the middle of the night.

田舎暮らしだと、買い物に出かけるのって大変だからさ。

ネットだとどんなものでも簡単に探せるしね。

今日注文したら、明日には自宅に品物が届くからいいよ。

ネットだと値段の比較ができるからいい。

ネットでの買い物は時間が節約できる。

ネットでの買い物は忙しい人にはピッタリだ。

描写表現　休日

休日を過ごす。

休日を家で過ごす。

家でくつろぐ。

描写表現　TV

テレビをつける。

リモコンを使ってテレビを操作する。

テレビのチャンネルを回す。

チャンネルを変える。

テレビのチャンネルを5にする。

7チャンネルを見る。

If you live in the country, going out to shop is a lot of trouble. / When you live in a rural area, going out to shop is a real hassle.

You can also search for any goods easily on the Internet. ⇨search for=find

It's good because you can order something today and it'll be delivered to your house tomorrow. ⇨it'll be delivered=it'll get

It's good because you can compare prices on the Net.

You can save time by buying online. ⇨online=on the Net

Internet shopping is perfect for busy people.

Descriptive expressions — Days off

I spend a day off.

I spend days off at home.

I relax at home.

Descriptive expressions — TV

I turn on the TV.

I use a remote control to operate the TV.

I switch the TV channels. / I surf the channels.
⇨switch=change

I change channels.

I go to Channel 5. ⇨go to=switch to

I watch Channel 7.

テレビニュースを見る。

テレビで映画を観る。

サッカーの試合を観る。

野球中継を観る。

お笑い番組を観る。

お菓子を食べながら歌番組を観る。

テレビを消す。

つぶやき表現　TV

テレビでも見るとしよう。

今9チャンネルでは何をやっているのかな。

どこかお笑い番組をやっているところはないかな。

つぶやき表現　面白い

この番組は面白いな。

だんだん面白くなってきたぞ。

彼は面白いな。

彼はどの番組にも出ている。

この番組が一番好きだ。

彼女はすごい人気がある。

この女性グループ歌手はひっぱりだこだ。

彼は若い女性たちにすごい人気だ。

つぶやき表現　コマーシャル

またコマーシャルか。

I watch TV news.

I watch movies on TV.

I watch a soccer game. / I watch a football match.

I watch a live baseball broadcast.

I watch a comedy show. ⇨ show =program

I watch a music program while eating sweets.

I turn off the TV. / I turn the TV off.

Mumblings — TV

Maybe I'll watch TV. ⇨ TV=television.

I wonder what's on Channel 9 now.

Maybe there's a comedy show on somewhere.

Mumblings — Interesting

This program's interesting. / This is an interesting show.

It's getting more and more interesting.

He's interesting. ⇨ interesting=funny

He's on every kind of program.

I like this program best./This is my favorite program.

She's very popular. ⇨ very=really

This group of female singers is in great demand.
⇨ is in great demand=is very popular

He's really popular with young girls.
⇨ popular with=popular among   ⇨ girls=women

Mumblings — Commercials

Another commercial, huh?

コマーシャルが多すぎる。

いいところでいつもコマーシャルだ。

つぶやき表現　面白い番組　　CD①②60

何か面白い番組はないかな。

この番組は面白そうだ。

9時から面白い番組があるぞ。

7チャンネルも観たいし、13チャンネルの番組も観たい。

3時から時代劇を観なくちゃ。

たしか1時30分からマラソンの中継があったはずだ。

もうすぐ13チャンネルでアメリカ西海岸特集が始まるぞ。

つぶやき表現　面白くない

最近はあまり面白い番組がないな。

今日は観たい番組がまったくない。

このドラマは全然面白くない。

この時間帯は観たい番組が全くないんだ。

このチャンネルは再放送ものが多い。

There are too many commercials.

They always have a commercial at the good places. / They always have a cut to a commercial at the best spots.

(Mumblings) Interesting programs

Isn't there something interesting on?

This program looks interesting.

There's an interesting program at nine o'clock.
⇨at=from

I wanna watch channel 7 and channel 13.

I have to watch a period movie from three o'clock. ⇨period movie=samurai drama

There was certainly supposed to be a live broadcast of a marathon from 1:30.

There's a special about the West Coast of America on channel 13 starting pretty soon.
⇨pretty soon=shortly

(Mumblings) Not interesting

These days, there aren't any interesting programs. ⇨These days=Nowadays ⇨programs=shows

There's no program I want to watch today. / There's absolutely nothing today.

This drama is totally uninteresting. ⇨totally=completely

There aren't any programs on at this hour that I want to watch.

This channel has a lot of re-runs. ⇨has=shows

描写表現　録画

テレビ番組を録画する。

お気に入りのテレビドラマを録画する。

今夜9時から放送の映画を録画する。

好きな女優が出る番組を録画する。

7時から始まる1時間もののホームドラマを留守録設定する。

描写表現　TVゲーム

テレビゲームをして午後を過ごす。

1人で野球のテレビゲームをする。

友人とサッカーのテレビゲームをして遊ぶ。

描写表現　音楽を聴く

音楽を聴く。

ポップミュージックを聞く。

コーヒーを飲みながらクラシック音楽を聴く。

カラオケをする。

カラオケで AKA の歌を歌う。

描写表現　写真を撮る

写真を撮る。

庭で咲いている花の写真を撮る。

花に止っている蝶の写真を撮る。

Descriptive expressions Recording

I record TV shows. ⇨shows=programs

I record my favorite TV dramas.

I'm gonna record a movie that's being broadcast at nine o'clock tonight.

I record programs that have an actress I like.

I record a one-hour sitcom from seven o'clock while I'm out. ⇨I'm out=I'm away from home

Descriptive expressions TV games

I spend afternoons playing video games. ⇨playing=doing

I play baseball video games by myself. ⇨by myself=alone

I play video soccer games with a friend.
⇨with a friend → with friends

Descriptive expressions Listening to music

I listen to music.

I listen to pop music.

I drink coffee while listening to classical music.

I do karaoke. / I go to karaoke.

I sing AKA songs at karaoke.

Descriptive expressions Taking pictures

I take pictures.

I take pictures of flowers blooming in the yard.
⇨yard=garden

I take pictures of butterflies stopping on the flowers.

近所の公園へ行って野鳥の写真を撮る。

兄に身分証明書用の写真を撮ってもらう。

写真をコンピュータに取り込む。

撮った花の写真をコンピュータで編集する。

描写表現　DVDを観る　　　　CD①②63

午後にビデオのレンタル屋へ行く。

借りてきた映画のDVDを観る。

つぶやき表現　役者について

この俳優は好きだな。

この女優はすごくチャーミングだ。

彼はいつ見てもカッコいい。

彼は演技がうまいな。

彼にはこの役がピッタリだ。

大統領の役をやらせたら彼は実にすばらしい。

彼の演技には説得力がある。

この俳優は大根役者だ。

彼女は演技が下手だね。

彼女はまるでセリフを単に読んでいるみたいだ。

つぶやき表現　ストーリー

この物語は実に感動的だ。

I take pictures of wild birds in a neighborhood park.

I have my brother take a photo of me for I.D.
⇨ brother=big brother; older brother; elder brother
⇨ I.D.=identification

I save pictures on my computer. ⇨ save pictures =store photos

I edit pictures of flowers that I took on my computer.

Descriptive expressions Watching DVDs

In the afternoon, I go to a video rental store.

I watch a DVD of a movie I rented. ⇨ rented=borrowed

Mumblings About actors

I like this actor.

This actress is very charming.

Whenever I see him he looks cool. ⇨ cool=sharp

He's a good performer, isn't he?

This role is perfect for him. / He's perfect for this role.

He is wonderful in the role of President.

His performance is convincing.

This actor is a ham.

She's a poor performer. ⇨ poor=bad

She looks like she's just reading her lines. ⇨ just=simply

Mumblings Story

This story is really moving. ⇨ moving=touching

このドラマは涙なくしてはとても観られない。

このストーリーは、余りにも悲しすぎる。

何度観てもこの映画はすばらしい。

俳優、演技、物語のどれを取っても、すべて最高だね。

このドラマの続きを早く観たい。

つぶやき表現　歌について　CD①②64

この曲を聴くと、いつも楽しくなる。

悲しいときとか、辛いときはいつもこの曲を聴くんだ。

気分が落ち込んだとき、この曲を聴くと元気になる。

彼女の歌を聴くと心が癒される。

車を運転するときは、いつも彼女の曲をかけるんだ。

描写表現　読書

小説を読む。

3日に1冊のペースで小説を読む。

小説を一気に読み終える。

小説を最初から最後まで読む。

夏目漱石の小説を途中まで読む。

I can't watch this drama without crying.

This story is so sad. ⇨ so sad=too sad

No matter how many times I watch it, this film is wonderful. ⇨ wonderful=marvelous

The actors, the performances, the story, whatever you choose they're all great.

I wanna see the sequel to this drama soon.

> Mumblings **About songs**

Whenever I listen to this song, it's fun.
⇨ it's fun=I have a good time

When I'm sad or miserable, I listen to this song.
⇨ I'm sad or miserable=I'm having a hard time

When I'm down, I listen to this song and feel better. ⇨ I'm down=I'm depressed; I'm feeling blue

When I listen to her songs it heals my heart.
⇨ it heals my heart=it soothes my spirit

I play her songs when I drive.

> Descriptive expressions **Reading**

I read novels.

I read novels at a rate of one every three days.
⇨ at a rate of=at a pace of

I finish a book all at once.

I read novels cover to cover.
⇨ cover to cover=from start to finish

I read Natsume Soseki's novels part way through.
⇨ part way through=half way through

283

漫画を週に 3 冊は読む。

毎週、漫画喫茶へ行って好きな漫画を読む。

One Point Lesson 「思い切って」の英語表現

　この日本語は英語でどう言ったらよいのでしょうか。このように英語で言いにくい日本語表現を扱う場合は、まず日本語の意味や同意の表現を考えてみるとよいでしょう。つまり、私たちが「思い切って〜」というときは、たいてい「勇気を出して〜」「勇気を奮い起こして〜」あるいは「大胆に〜」といった意味合いで使っているはずです。
　そこで、困難や危険を恐れることなく、ある事柄や問題に立ち向かう精神を表す英語 courage を使って、「勇気を奮い起こして」といった意味を表すイディオム、すなわち pluck up one's courage、summon up courage、gather one's courage を用いると問題解決です。なお、I didn't have the heart to tell her his death.（私は彼女に彼の死を告げる勇気などとてもなかった）のように have the heart to do という表現もありますが、この場合は通例、否定文、疑問文で用いられます。

One Point Lesson pupil と student

　日本では大学生は「学生」、中学、高校では「生徒」、そして小学校では「児童」あるいは「生徒」と呼ばれています。一方、アメリカでは中学、高校、大学生を student、小学生を pupil と呼んでいますが、近年では小学校の生徒についても student が使われています。なお、イギリスでは student は通例、大学生のみに適応され、小、中、高校生は pupil です。
　ちなみに、「まじめな学生」は an earnest student、「優秀な学生」は an excellent student、「優等生」は an honor student、「良い学生」は a good student、「勤勉な学生」は a hardworking student、「成績がずば抜けた学生」は an outstanding student、「理解力の優れた学生」は a quick student、a quick-learning student、「理解力の弱い学生」は a slow student、a slow-learning student、「学力の低い学生」は a poor student、a weak student、「平均的な学生」は an average student、「模範的な学生」は a model student です。そして「大学の学部生は an undergraduate student、「大学院生」は a graduate student とします。

I read at least three comic books a week.
⇨ comic books=manga

I go to a manga coffee shop every week and read my favorite manga. ⇨ manga coffee shop=manga tea room ⇨ my favorite manga=manga I like

One Point Lesson　名刺は英語で business card

　私たちはビジネスシーンで自己紹介したり、人に紹介される際に、通例、名刺を交換しますが、その「名刺」を表す英語には business card、calling card（アメリカ）、visiting card（イギリス）、card などがあります。
　これらの違いは business card が業務用の名刺、calling card、visiting card が個人用の名刺を指しています。ちなみに、胸に付ける名札は He has a name plate on his chest.（彼は胸に名札を付けている）といった具合に name plate、衣服や荷物、カバンなどに付ける「名札」「荷札」は nametag、name tag といいます。

One Point Lesson　すねをかじる

　「すねをかじる」とは「居候になる」とか「人のやっかいになる」という意味ですね。これに相当する英語表現は I intend to sponge off my family for a while.（しばらく家族のやっかいになるつもりだ）のように、人のよさ、親切、友情などに付け込んで利益などをスポンジのように「吸収する、吸い取る」を表す sponge を用いて sponge off、sponge on とします。
　ただし、この表現は He sponges on her for money.（彼は彼女に金をたかる）といった具合に、しばしば軽蔑的な意味合いで使われます。類似したものに He is still living off his parents.（彼はいまだ両親のすねをかじっている）、live off、He is depending on his parents for food and clothing.（彼は両親に衣食の世話になっている）のように、生活、扶養、援助などを「頼る、依存する」を表す depend on、また depend の形容詞を用いて be dependent on などがあります。

描写表現　外食　　CD①②65

外食する。

今日は家で食べないで、外へ食べに出る。

フランス料理の店を探す。

レストランへ行く。

近くのエスニック料理店へ行く。

近くにできた中華料理の店へ行く。

行きつけのイタリア料理の店へ行く。

イタリア料理の店に予約を入れる。

2人分の席を予約する。

描写表現　注文

メニューを頼む。

メニューを見る。

料理を注文する。

コース料理を注文する。

一品料理を注文する。

野菜料理を注文する。

肉料理を注文する。

お勧め料理を尋ねる。

地元の料理を尋ねる。

つぶやき表現　注文

今日のお勧めはなんだろう。

Descriptive expressions Eating out

I eat out. / I go out to eat.

I won't eat at home today, I'll go out to eat.

I look for a French restaurant.

I go to a restaurant.

I go to a nearby ethnic restaurant.

I go to a new nearby Chinese restaurant.

I go to my favorite Italian restaurant.

I make a reservation at an Italian restaurant.

I make a reservation for two. / I reserve a table for two.

Descriptive expressions Ordering

I order a menu. / I ask for a menu.

I look at a menu. ⇨ a → the

I order food.

I order a food course menu. ⇨ course menu=set menu

I order one dish. ⇨ dish=serving

I order vegetables. / I order vegetarian food.

I order a meat dish. / I order meat.

I ask about recommended dishes.

I ask about local dishes. ⇨ dishes=foods

Mumblings Ordering

What's today's special? / What do they recommend today?

肉料理は苦手なんだ。

今日は野菜中心の料理にしよう。

どちらかというと魚料理がいいな。

描写表現　飲み物　　CD①②66

最初にシャンペンを注文する。

ワインをグラスで注文する。

高級ワインを1本注文する。

グラスにビールをつぐ。

彼のグラスにビールをつぐ。

乾杯する。

健康を願ってビールで乾杯する。

再会を祝して乾杯する。

彼女の誕生日を祝って乾杯する。

ビールを一気に飲み干す。

日本酒を一口すする。

日本酒を熱燗でチビチビやる。

描写表現　食べる

サラダにドレッシングをかける。

スパゲティに粉チーズをかける。

ステーキをナイフで切る。

スープを飲む。

料理を食べる。

I don't like meat.

I'll mainly eat veggies today.

I guess I'll have fish.

Descriptive expressions — Drinks/Beverages

I order champagne first.

I order a glass of wine.

I order a bottle of fine wine.

I pour beer into a glass.

I pour beer into his glass.

We make a toast.

We drink a toast with beer for health reasons.
⇨ for health reasons=for our health

We drink a celebratory toast at a reunion.

We drink a toast to her birthday.

I drink a beer down in one gulp. / I drink a beer bottoms up.

I sip a mouthful of sake. ⇨ sake=Japanese sake

I drink hot sake little by little.

Descriptive expressions — Eat

I put dressing on a salad.

I sprinkle powdered cheese on spaghetti.

I cut steak with a knife.

I eat soup.

I eat food.

料理を味見する。

ステーキを噛む。

ステーキを飲み込む。

アイスクリームをスプーンで食べる。

描写表現　その他の表現　CD①②67

禁煙席を要求する。

禁煙席に座る。

窓側の席に座る。

通りに面した席を要求する。

角の席を選ぶ。

席を交換してもらう。

おしぼりで手をふく。

描写表現　レストラン

レストランは混んでいる。

レストランはガラガラだ。

レストランは客がまばらだ。

レストランは急に混みだした。

レストランの雰囲気が良い。

レストランは高級感にあふれている。

レストランの雰囲気が安っぽい。

描写表現　サービス　CD①②68

サービスが良い。

I taste the food

I chew a steak.

I swallow some steak.

I eat ice cream with a spoon.

Descriptive expressions Other expressions

I ask for a non-smoking seat. ⇨ non-smoking seat=non-smoking table

I sit at a non-smoking seat. ⇨ seat=table

I sit at a window seat. ⇨ window seat=window table

I ask for a seat with a view of the street. / I ask for a seat facing the street.

I choose a corner seat.

I get someone to change seats.

I wipe hands with a wet washcloth.

Descriptive expressions Restaurants

The restaurant is crowded. ⇨ crowded=packed

The restaurant is empty.

There are few customers in the restaurant.

The restaurant quickly filled up. ⇨ quickly=suddenly

The restaurant has a good atmosphere. ⇨ good=nice

The restaurant has a high class feeling. / The restaurant feels really high class.

The restaurant has a cheap atmosphere.

Descriptive expressions Service

The service is good.

この店のサービスは最低だ。

ボーイの態度が良い。

ウエイトレスがとても親切だ。

従業員のマナーが悪い。

つぶやき表現 レストランについて

この店の雰囲気は良くないね。

店員の態度は最低だね。

この店はいつ来てもお客でいっぱいだ。

この時間はいつも満席だ。

また満席か。

30分待ちなんてごめんだね。

相席はいやだね。

彼女と2人だけで座りたいんだ。

描写表現 その他の表現　　　CD①②69

ナイフとフォークを使って食べる。

ナイフで肉を切る。

The service at this restaurant is terrible.
⇨terrible=sucks

The waiter has a good attitude. ⇨waiter=bus boy

The waitress is very kind.

The staff's manners are bad. / The employees are bad-mannered.

> Mumblings About restaurants

The atmosphere in this restaurant is bad.
⇨in=of ⇨bad=no good

The store staff's attitude is terrible. ⇨terrible=really bad

Whenever I come to this store it's full of customers.

It's always full at this time. / The seats are always full at this time. ⇨seats=tables

Full again? / Oh, it's full again.

I'm not gonna wait for thirty minutes.
⇨wait for thirty minutes=wait thirty minutes

I don't wanna share a table with someone. / I don't want to share a seat with anybody.

I want a table for two, for just her and me. / I want a table for just the two of us, her and me.
⇨her and me=she and I

> Descriptive expressions Other expressions

I eat with a knife and fork. / I eat using a knife and fork.

I cut meat with a knife.

293

ナイフを変えてもらう。

フォークが汚れているので、変えてもらう。

箸を持ってきてもらう。

割り箸を割る。

割り箸を使う。

描写表現　支払

勘定を頼む。

支払をする。

支払いをテーブルですませる。

カードで支払う。

食事代を現金で支払う。

2人分の食事代を払う。

みんなにディナーをおごる。

割り勘にする。

食事代を相手に払ってもらう。

描写表現　チップ　　　　　　　　　　　CD①②70

チップをあげる

ウエイトレスにチップを渡す。

I get a new knife. / I have them replace the knife. ⇨ new knife=different knife ⇨ replace=change

The fork's dirty, so I get another one. ⇨ another =a new

I have some chopsticks brought. / I have someone bring chopsticks.

I split disposable wooden chopsticks.
⇨ disposable wooden chopsticks=disposable chopsticks; throwaway chopsticks; half-split chopstics

I use disposable chopsticks.

> **Descriptive expressions** Paying the bill / Paying the tab

I ask for the bill. ⇨ bill=tab

I pay the bill. / I pay up.

I pay the bill at the table.

I pay by credit card. / I pay by plastic.

I pay the bill for the food in cash. ⇨ in cash=with cash

I pay for two. / I pay for two meals. ⇨ meals=orders

I treat everyone to dinner. / I pick up the tab for all of us. ⇨ pick up=pay

I split the bill. / I share the tab. / We go Dutch.

I have the other person pay the bill for the meal. ⇨ person=party

> **Descriptive expressions** Tip

I give a tip. / I leave a tip.

I hand a tip to the waitress. / I tip the waitress.
⇨ hand= give

食事代の 10% をチップとして払う。

チップを出さない。

ウエーターの態度が悪いからチップを出さない。

つぶやき表現　**持ち金**

合計いくらになるかな？

財布にいくら入っていたっけ？

今日はあまりお金を持っていないんだ。

今月のこづかいはもうほとんど残っていない。

まずい、1 万円しか持っていない。

お金が足りない。

勘定が間違っている。

おつりが間違っている。

SOS 表現

つぶやき表現　**頼んでない**　　　　　　　　CD①2 71

この料理は頼んでいないぞ。

注文していない料理が来た。

I give a tip of ten percent of the bill. / I tip ten percent. ⇨give=leave

I don't tip.

The waiter's attitude was bad, so I don't leave a tip. ⇨bad=sucked

(Mumblings) **Money in the wallet**

How much is the bill?

How much do I have in my wallet? / How much is there in my billfold?

I don't have much money today.
⇨I don't have=I'm not carrying

I don't have much left of my pocket money this month. ⇨pocket money=allowance

Oh no! I have only ten thousand yen. / I only have 10,000 yen.

I don't have enough money.

The bill's wrong. / There's a mistake on the tab.
⇨tab=check

The change is wrong. / He gave me the wrong change.

SOS expressions

(Mumblings) **I didn't order**

I didn't order this food. ⇨food=dish

Food came that I didn't order.
⇨I didn't order=I hadn't ordered

297

注文した料理が間違っている。

注文した料理がまだ来ない。

描写表現　食べ物について

スープが冷めている。

肉が固い。

料理の中に変なものが入っている。

サラダに虫が入っている。

つぶやき表現　その他の表現

もうお腹いっぱいだ。

もうこれ以上は食べられない。

これだけじゃあ物足りないな。

もっと食べたい。

One Point Lesson　in the world について

　この表現は This is the highest mountain in the world.（これは世界一高い山です）のように「世界で」の意味ですが、イディオムとして使われた場合は全く別の意味を表します。たとえば、What in the world are you doing here?（君、ここで一体何をしているんだね）といった具合に、疑問文で使われ、疑問を強めて「一体全体」を意味します。同意のものとして on earth、少々荒っぽい表現 the devil、in the devil、the hell などがあります。

　なお、in the world は I never in the world would have said such a thing.（私ならそんなことは言わなかっただろう）のように、否定文で否定の意を強め「全く」の意でも頻繁に使われます。

They mistook the food I ordered. / They made a mistake about what I ordered.
⇨ about what I ordered=on my order

The food I ordered hasn't come yet.

Descriptive expressions **About Food**

The soup's cold.

The meat's tough. ⇨ tough=chewy

Something strange is in the food.

There are bugs in the salad. ⇨ bugs=insects

Mumblings **Other expressions**

I'm already full. / I'm stuffed.

I can't eat another bite. / I can't eat any more than this.

This isn't enough. / Only this won't be enough.
⇨ Only=Just

I wanna eat more. ⇨ eat more=eat some more

One Point Lesson　make it について

　この表現は I made it to the last train.（最終列車に間に合った）とか I'm sorry I won't be able to make it to your party.（残念だが、君のパーティに行けそうもない）といった具合に「どうにか間に合う、たどり着く、やり遂げる」などの意で使われる便利なイディオム。そのため「やったぜ！」としたい場合は、これを使って I made it!、「彼は商売で成功するだろう」を英訳したい場合は He will make it in business. とすればオーケー。

Chapter 5 夜

描写表現 帰宅　　　　　　　　　　　　　CD①②72

帰宅する。

定刻に帰宅する。

今日は夜10時に帰宅する。

自宅の駐車場に車を停める。

車から出て、玄関まで歩く。

玄関のドアベルを鳴らす。

玄関のカギを開ける。

ドアノブを回し、ドアを開け、家に入る。

玄関で靴を脱ぐ。

スリッパをはく。

服を着替える。

背広からホームウエアに着替える。

描写表現 夜食

夜食を作る。

夜食にラーメンを食べる。

小腹が空いたので、夜食に焼きおにぎりを食べる。

Night

朝・午前

Descriptive expressions Coming home / Getting back home

I come home.

I go home at the scheduled time.

I get home at ten o'clock tonight.

I park my car in the residential parking lot.
⇨park=stop

昼

I get out of the car and walk to my front door.
⇨front door=front entrance

I ring the doorbell.

I unlock the front door.

I turn the doorknob, open the door and go into the house.

午後

I take off my shoes at the entrance.
⇨at the entrance=in the foyer

I put on slippers. ⇨put on=wear

I change clothes.

夕方

I change from a suit to house clothes.

Descriptive expressions Midnight snack

I fix a night meal. ⇨night meal=midnight snack

I have ramen for the night meal. ⇨have=eat

Stomach's empty, so I eat a toasted rice ball at night. ⇨Stomach's empty=Tummy's empty ⇨toasted=grilled

夜

301

夜食にカロリーの少ないものを食べる。

描写表現　その他の表現　　　CD①②73

携帯電話を充電する。

日記をつける。

1日の出来事を日記に書く。

今日、思ったこと、考えたことをノートにメモする。

明日、着ていく服を準備する。

描写表現　化粧落とし

化粧を落とす。

クレンジングを使って化粧をしっかり落とす。

就寝前にメイクを落としてからぬるま湯で洗顔する。

肌にうるおいを与えるために化粧水をつける。

肌荒れを防ぐためにクリームを塗る。

描写表現　風呂　　　CD①②74

湯を沸かす。

バスタブに湯を入れる。

風呂に入浴剤を入れる。

I eat low calorie food for midnight snack.

Descriptive expressions — Other expressions

I charge my cell phone.

I write a diary.

I write what happened for the day in the diary.

I write a memo in a notebook about what I felt and thought about.

I get the clothes to wear tomorrow ready.

Descriptive expressions — Removing make-up

I remove make-up.

I use cleansing cream to completely remove make-up.

After removing make-up, I wash my face with warm water before going to bed.
⇨ before going to bed=before I go to bed; before I sleep

I put lotion on my skin to moisturize it.

I apply cream to prevent rough skin.

Descriptive expressions — Bath

I run a bath. / I fill the bathtub.

I run warm water into the bathtub. / I fill the tub with warm water. ⇨ I run=I put

I put bath salts into the tub.

バラの香りの入浴剤を入れる。

服を脱ぐ。

浴室に入る。

体を洗う。

体の隅々までボディソープで良く洗う。

描写表現　シャンプー

シャンプーする。

髪にコンディショナーをつける。

コンディショナーをきれいに洗い流す。

湯につかる前に頭を洗う。

描写表現　湯に浸かる

全身に湯をかける。

湯につかる。

42度の湯につかる。

少し熱めの湯に入る。

ぬるま湯の風呂に入る。

風呂に入ってゆっくり肩まで浸かる。

半身浴する。

描写表現　風呂から出る

バスタブから出る。

I put in rose fragrance oil.
⇨ rose fragrance oil=rose fragrance salts

I get undressed. / I take off my clothes.

I get into the bath. ⇨ bath=tub

I wash my body.

I wash every part of my body well with body lotion. ⇨ every part of=every square inch of

> Descriptive expressions **Shampoo**

I shampoo.

I put conditioner in my hair.

I wash the conditioner out of my hair thoroughly.

I wash my head before soaking in the bath.
⇨ head → hair → face

> Descriptive expressions **Soaking in warm water**

I pour warm water all over my body.

I soak in the warm water.

I soak in 42 degree warm water.

I soak in a little warmer water.

I get in a tepid bath. ⇨ tepid=lukewarm

I get in the bath and slowly soak in shoulder deep.

I bathe half my body.

> Descriptive expressions **Getting out of bath**

I get out of the bathtub.

バスタオルで体をふく。

頭にトニックをふりかける。

頭皮を指でマッサージする。

肌の手入れをする。

ストレッチをする。

描写表現　布団

布団を押入れから出す。

布団を畳の上に敷く。

目覚まし時計を朝6時30分にセットする。

布団の中に入る。

ベッドに入る。

ベッドで横になる。

描写表現　睡眠

すぐ眠りに落ちる。

ベッドに入ったとたん、眠りに落ちる。

考え事をしていて眠れない。

眠ろうとすればするほど眠れない。

体は眠っているのに、脳は起きている。

眠りが浅い。

ぐっすり眠る。

I dry off with a bath towel. / I wipe my body with a bath towel.

I sprinkle tonic on my head.

I massage my scalp with my fingers.

I do skin care.

I stretch.

Descriptive expressions Futon

I take a futon out of the closet.

I spread the futon on the tatami mat.

I set the alarm clock for 6:30 a.m.
⇨ a.m.=in the morning

I get into the futon. ⇨ into=under

I get into bed.

I lie in bed.

Descriptive expressions Sleep

I fall asleep soon. ⇨ soon=quickly.

I fall asleep as soon as I get into bed. / I go to sleep as soon as my head touches the pillow.

I can't sleep, thinking about things.

The more I try to sleep the less sleepy I get. / I can't sleep from trying so hard to sleep.

My body's asleep, but my brain is awake.

I sleep shallowly.

I sleep well. / I sleep like a baby.

描写表現　夢　　　　　　　　　　　　　　　　　　　　　CD①②77

夢を見る。

真夜中に悪夢にうなされる。

夢を見たが、どんな夢だったか思い出せない。

宝くじが１億円当たった夢をみる。

描写表現　**その他の表現**

夜更かしをする。

徹夜で勉強をする。

横向きで寝る。

上を向いて寝る。

うつ伏せになって寝る。

何度も寝返りをうつ。

いびきをかく。

歯ぎしりをする。

Descriptive expressions — Dream

I dream.

I have a nightmare in the middle of the night.

I had a dream but I can't remember what I dreamt.

I dreamt I won a hundred million yen in the lottery.

Descriptive expressions — Other expressions

I stay up late. / I go to bed late.

I study all night. / I stay up all night studying.

I sleep on my side.

I sleep facing up. / I sleep on my back.

I sleep face-down. / I sleep on my tummy.

I turn over in bed many times.

I snore.

I gnash. / I grind my teeth.

英語アプリで本書の音声を無料で聴くことができます

AI 英語教材アプリ abceed
（株式会社 Globee 提供）
① アプリストアで「abceed」をダウンロード。
② アプリを立ち上げ、本書の名前を検索して音声を使用。

　abceed アプリの登録・操作方法についてはネットで「abceed アカウントの登録 / 編集方法」で検索してサイトへ。
　それでもわからない場合は【abceed サポート窓口】
support@globeejphelp.zendesk.com　へお問い合わせください。

英語アプリ mikan
① アプリストアで「mikan」をダウンロード。
② アプリを立ち上げ、「教材一覧」の検索バーで本書の名前を検索。
③ 音声ボタン（♪）より、音声を再生。

https://mikan.link/beret

アプリに関するお問い合わせについては弊社では対応しておりません。各アプリのお問い合わせ窓口にご連絡ください。

●著者紹介

曽根田 憲三（そねだ けんぞう）

立教大学大学院修了。相模女子大学名誉教授。UCLA（カリフォルニア大学ロサンゼルス校）客員研究員（'94、'97、'00）。アメリカ映画文化学会会長、映画英語アカデミー学会会長。著書に『今日のアメリカ小説』『アメリカ文学と映画』（開文社出版）、『CD BOOK 教室で使う英語表現集』『CD BOOK 暮らしの英会話表現辞典』『CD BOOK シンプルな英語で日本を紹介する』『書きたいことがパッと書ける英語表現集』（ベレ出版）、『日常生活ですぐに使える英語表現集』「昔ばなしで英会話シリーズ」『桃太郎』『かぐや姫』『つるのおんがえし』（勉誠出版）など。なお、『風と共に去りぬ』『第三の男』『シャレード』『欲望という名の電車』（スクリーンプレイ事業部）など、数十冊のアメリカ映画シナリオ対訳本を含めると、その数は約160冊に及ぶ。

Bruce Perkins（ブルース・パーキンス）

オハイオ州立大学大学院修了。元相模女子大学教授、外務省研修所講師、アメリカ映画文化学会理事。著書に『CD BOOK 教室で使う英語表現集』『CD BOOK 暮らしの英会話表現辞典』『CD BOOK シンプルな英語で日本を紹介する』『書きたいことがパッと書ける英語表現集』（ベレ出版）など多数。

CDの内容
- 時間…DISC1 67分00秒 / DISC2 60分24秒
- ナレーション…Howard Colefield / Bianca Allen

CD BOOK 一日のすべてを英語で表現してみる

2013年10月25日 初版発行	
2025年10月29日 第12版発行	
著者	曽根田憲三　ブルース・パーキンス
カバーデザイン	田栗克己
イラスト	いげためぐみ

© Kenzo Soneda, Bruce Perkins 2013. Printed in Japan

発行者	内田真介
発行・発売	ベレ出版 〒162-0832 東京都新宿区岩戸町12レベッカビル TEL 03-5225-4790　FAX 03-5225-4795 ホームページ https://www.beret.co.jp/
印刷	三松堂株式会社
製本	根本製本株式会社

落丁本・乱丁本は小社編集部あてにお送りください。送料小社負担にてお取り替えします。
本書の無断複写は著作権法上での例外を除き禁じられています。
購入者以外の第三者による本書のいかなる電子複製も一切認められておりません。

ISBN978-4-86064-372-0 C2082　　　　　　　　　編集担当　綿引ゆか

[音声 DL 付] 自己紹介からはじめてどんどん仲良くなるための英会話表現集

曽根田憲三 著

四六並製／定価 2200 円（税込）■ 280 頁
ISBN978-4-86064-760-5 C2082

自己紹介は、人と出会って、話を広げて、楽しく、お互いのことを知って友情や信頼関係へと発展していくきっかけになります。本書では、最初の挨拶から名前、出身地、趣味などの基本的な表現から、性格、夢、将来、価値観についての表現まで、円滑なコミュニケーションに欠かせない表現を豊富に紹介します。文法、語彙と表現についての丁寧な解説も付いています。実践的な英語学習を進め、たくさん友だちを作りましょう！

[音声 DL 付] 一日の会話のすべてを英語にしてみる

曽根田憲三／上原寿和子 著

四六並製／定価 2200 円（税込）■ 368 頁
ISBN978-4-86064-601-1 C2082

起きてから寝るまでの一日に交わす会話を全部英語にして紹介します。「まだ寝てるの？」「もうちょっと」、「明日忙しい？」「午後なら大丈夫」「今日はいい天気だね」「久しぶりじゃない？」というように日常会話でよくあるやりとりがたくさん集めてあります。会話形式なので、話しかけ表現にあいづち表現、質問表現に返しの表現、とセットで覚えることができます。また、決まり表現やイディオムが頻出するため表現の幅も広がります。ダウンロード音声には本書にある会話表現のすべてを収録。ネイティブの自然な英語を聞くことで、正しい発音が身につき、暗唱トレーニングにも活用できます。

[音声 DL 付]〈50 音順〉一日の会話で使う動詞のすべてを英語にしてみる

曽根田憲三 著

四六並製／定価 2200 円（税込）■ 464 頁
ISBN978-4-86064-663-9 C2082

人、モノ、場所を表わす名詞は大切ですが、意思の疎通を図るためには、どうするのか、どう思っているの、どうなっているのかを伝えるための「動詞」が必要です。本書では、日常会話の中で頻繁に使われている、基本的な日本語の動詞を 50 音順に並べ、会話でよく使われる表現と一緒に紹介します。「会う」で see と meet の違いがわかり、「合う」で「似合う」は suit、サイズが「合う」は fit など、違いと使い分けを理解しながら覚えていくことができます。